The Washington Papers/93 ~~DISCARDED~~ Volume X

SOVIET STRATEGY IN LATIN AMERICA

ROBERT S. LEIKEN 1939-

Foreword by William D. Rogers

Published with The Center for
Strategic and International Studies,
Georgetown University, Washington, D.C.

PRAEGER

PRAEGER SPECIAL STUDIES • PRAEGER SCIENTIFIC

Library of Congress Cataloging in Publication Data

Leiken, Robert S., 1939–
    Soviet strategy in Latin America.

    (The Washington papers, ISSN 0278-937X ; v. 10,
#93)
    Includes bibliographical references.
    1. Latin America—Strategic aspects. 2. Soviet
Union—Military policy. I. Title. II. Series.
UA602.3.L44   1982   327.4708   82-9788
ISBN 0-03-062017-1   AACR2

The *Washington Papers* are written under the auspices of The Center
for Strategic and International Studies (CSIS), Georgetown University,
and published with CSIS by Praeger Publishers. The views expressed in these
papers are those of the authors and not necessarily those of The Center.

Published in 1982 by Praeger Publishers
CBS Educational and Professional Publishing
a Division of CBS Inc.
521 Fifth Avenue, New York, New York 10175 U.S.A.

Printed in the United States of America

Contents

Foreword

Robert Leiken's contribution to the *Washington Papers* keeps this series by the Center for Strategic and International Studies at the forefront of American public policy. There has been ample rhetoric on Soviet intentions in this hemisphere. But two successive administrations have demonstrated that precise analysis of our interests in Latin America, and of the ways in which Soviet policy affects those interests, is no easier for Republicans than for Democrats. Former Secretary of State Alexander Haig, in particular, seemed to be saying in his less guarded moments that the conflict in El Salvador was only an extension of the superpower competition, that it was manipulated by outside forces, that its "source" was Cuba, and that a cessation of external support for the guerrillas by the Havana/Moscow cabal was both necessary and sufficient to stop the fighting. That this is not the most brilliant analysis of Central American instability has been made all too obvious by what has happened and not happened—by the successes and failures of American foreign policy in Central America in recent years. An effort to submit these questions to serious and systematic study is therefore timely and welcome. Particularly so if that study is informed with an appreciation of the complexity of current events and of their historic background, as this one is.

Leiken begins with an unromantic view of Soviet aspirations. Not all will agree that "armed struggle has become the cardinal point of Soviet Latin American doctrines," or that this is a "Latin American echo" of the "Soviet global offensive"—an offensive begun some years earlier in Africa, Asia, and the Middle East. And Leiken himself points out that "Soviet endorsement of armed struggle in Latin America is not absolute . . . the Soviets are pursuing dual tactics." But it is true enough that Anastasio Somoza's overthrow burst like a bombshell on Soviet consciousness, disclosing unsuspected revolutionary possibilities within Central America, and that this event was surely decisive in persuading Moscow to take a new look at his Central American opportunities.

It is also true enough that during the 1970s there was a sea change in the Soviet relationship with Cuba. Strained in the mid-1960s, that relationship has warmed in recent years as the two have converged in their views of the strategic openings in the Third World. And this has been accompanied by the massive Soviet rearming of the Cuban military and the deployment of Cuban armed forces in Africa and the Middle East.

There is a limit to most generalizations, and there is certainly a limit to a Soviet strategy based on armed struggle in Latin America. In the major countries armed struggle is just not a live option today. Violent conflict is the order of the day in much of Central America—on which Leiken concentrates—and with it, the open moral—and muffled material—support from Havana and Moscow for the insurgents. But Mexico and Brazil represent, at best, a trading opportunity for the Soviets; this is also clearly the case in Argentina, the source of much of the wheat imported into Russia today, even after the Falklands/Malvinas crisis. Furthermore, a more aggressive strategy, though it seems to have inspired a new congeniality between Cuba and Russia, has been counterproductive elsewhere in the hemisphere. Although Soviet interests have been enhanced in Central

America and Grenada, they have suffered in Panama, Jamaica, Venezuela, and elsewhere. In consequence, as Leiken points out, "Cuba's diplomatic relations with Latin America have been virtually reduced to Argentina, Brazil, Mexico, Grenada, Guyana, and Panama." Although he also points out its position may have been "partially repaired by its boisterous support of Argentina" during the Malvinas crisis. The reason for this is not ideology but nationalism. Leiken makes a contribution to the national discourse by emphasizing that "the resistance is not to Marxism or to socialism per se, but to encroachments on national sovereignty." This is his central insight.

Latin America—on this one matter a broader generalization is possible—seeks independence and freedom from intervention beyond all else. Different countries experiment with different ways of arranging their domestic order and responding to the international economic crisis. But all are committed to the preservation of their own independence and integrity.

Thus the elegance of Leiken's analysis, in welcome contrast to so much of the current debate in official Washington. He acknowledges that "the Soviet global offensive" came late to Latin America, when violence in Central America made it seem "propitious." And, just as the revolutions in Central America did not begin in Moscow, so any effort to submit them to Soviet control will inevitably "encounter popular resistance." The answer to a lunge by the Soviets for hegemony is not a counterhegemony. The United States policy response must include, as he tidily puts it, "relations of mutual economic benefit, an even-handed human rights policy . . . military cooperation against external threats to national sovereignty but not against internal popular opposition, and extensive political consultation and coordination."

All in all, Leiken has contributed importantly to the

general understanding of Central American events and Soviet designs. And his timing could hardly be better.

William D. Rogers
Former Assistant Secretary
of State for Inter-American Affairs

July 1982

Preface

This paper considers Soviet-Cuban activities in Latin America in the light of evolving Soviet political doctrine. It explores the significance of the shift in Moscow's general policy for Latin America from a "peaceful transition to socialism" to support for armed struggle in a growing number of Latin American countries.

Space limitations confine our examination of Soviet practice mainly to Central America and the Caribbean—where local conditions have presented Moscow with convenient targets of opportunity. As a result we have largely omitted a whole dimension of Soviet Latin American strategy: the securing of a military presence in the southern cone with tactics of accommodation and peaceful penetration in Peru and, especially, Argentina.

For this Soviet objective the Malvinas crisis has been a windfall. This study was completed before its outbreak, but even at this early stage of the crisis (May 1982), it is clear that Moscow will be its major beneficiary. For the first time since the Afghanistan invasion, Moscow can appear as the natural ally of the anticolonialists. Already Cuba's diplomatic position in Latin America, set back by recent Cuban adventurism, has been partially repaired by its boisterous support for Argentina (including offers of military assistance). U.S. dismissal of what Latin America regarded as U.S. Rio Pact obligations to Argentina has made U.S. exhortations for "collective security" against Soviet-Cuban expansionism sound hypocritical to Latin ears. This kind of environment is conducive to the realization of Soviet objectives in Latin America, but it is also a nourishing one for Latin American nationalism—which is, as we shall argue throughout this paper, the surest bulwark against Soviet penetration.

For their help with this study I thank Leslie Hunter for her outstanding research assistance, Susan Chodakewitz for careful double-checking of citations, and Ruth Udell for research and typing. I also thank Morris Rothenberg, Angela Stent, Horacio Crespo, Pedro Salas, Adolfo Aguilar Zinser, Horacio Lofredo, Georges Fauriol, Barry Rubin, Joseph Circincione, Francisco Perez Rangel, and Lorenzo Canizares for information, advice, and criticism. I am also indebted to the Tinker Foundation and the Rockefeller Foundation for their interest and support.

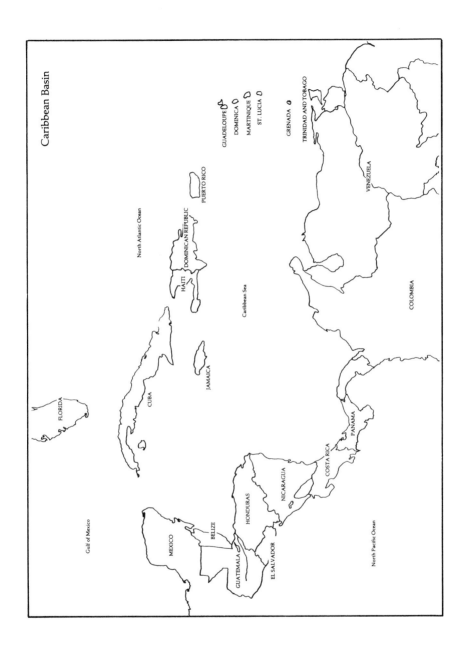

Caribbean Basin

South America

1

Latin America and the Superpowers: An Era of Change

Since the Spanish and Portuguese conquests in the six-teenth century, political and economic independence has been Latin America's driving goal, one it shares with other Third World countries. Although most Latin American countries gained formal political sovereignty more than a century before the rest of the colonized world, only the con-ditions of the struggle against foreign domination were changed.

For most of the twentieth century, the United States, enjoying an ascendency unmatched since the Spaniards, has been considered the lion in the path of Latin American self-determination. The United States did not abstain from military intervention and occupation, but it generally pre-ferred less direct methods: forming and assisting military juntas, training and financing local armies and police, back-ing constitutional "revisions," forging coercive military treaties, and applying a host of economic and political pres-sures and sanctions. These tactics illustrate what has been called the U.S. "hegemonic presumption"—that Latin America was but an exotic extension of the "frontier" required to shape its economic and political life to American tastes.[1]

For centuries, Latin American economies have been geared to supplying primary products to overseas markets. Although generating a certain uneven development, this has led to a structural deformation of the productive system, technological and financial dependency, and unemployment on a scale inconceivable in the developed countries. Cast in the mold of export economies, Latin American countries, attempting to industrialize, had instead to expand primary exports to acquire sufficient foreign exchange. The effort was made doubly difficult by unfavorable international terms of trade. Low export earnings needed to be supplemented by loans from the advanced countries (especially the United States), adding financial to technological and commercial dependence. Moreover, to stay competitive with other Third World primary producers, Latin American governments resisted unionization, kept wages down, and compelled the peasantry to sell at low prices to subsidize poorly-paid urban workers. Thus, external dependency reinforced internal poverty, backwardness, and underdevelopment.

In the eyes of many Latin Americans the problems of their dependent economic structure were compounded by cultural dependency. A steady stream of American music, movies, television and radio programs, magazines, press services, research projects, curriculum development programs, scholarships, Boy Scouts, Lion Clubs, and the latest styles of American clothing, restaurants, automobiles, and sports seemed to sweep away local and national traditions, leaving a country as bare as it was poor.

The international relations of Latin American countries also appeared "made in the USA," as they obediently broke diplomatic relations with the Soviet Union after World War II, lined up behind the Marshall Plan, lent support to South

Korea and Israel, and acceded to the isolation of the People's Republic of China (PRC) and the embargo of Cuba. The Cuban revolution in 1959, however, marked the beginning of the end of the U.S. era in Latin American history. Although the United States helped persuade most member governments of the Organization of American States (OAS) to cancel diplomatic and economic relations with Cuba in the early 1960s, it could not prevent the Cuban revolution from becoming a symbol for the resurgent popular nationalism of the years after the U.S. invasion of the Dominican Republic in 1965.

After 1965, Inter-American military cooperation retreated before the political tides originating in the universities and churches and before the rising national pride of an emerging industrial and financial middle class. While students mobilized behind slogans of "Yankee go home," anti-U.S. sentiment was pervading the armed forces as well, especially the younger, university-educated officers. From Brazil and Peru came national security doctrines that held social integration and economic development as the foundation of stability, not U.S. military assistance. In the universities and international organizations theories arose attributing Latin American underdevelopment and backwardness mainly to dependence on Spain, England, and, especially now, the United States. This reaction against "dependent capitalism" promoted by the United States lent socialism prestige and cast Cuba and the Soviet Union in a favorable light. U.S. counterinsurgency efforts in Vietnam and in Latin America and U.S. backing of oppressive regimes in the Third World persuaded many Latin Americans that the United States was the enemy of self-determination and the Soviet Union their natural ally.

By the late 1960s, the movement to nationalize foreign holdings was sweeping through Latin America—first southward along the Andes from Peru down to Chile, Bolivia, and Argentina, then northward in the 1970s to Guyana, Venezuela, and the Caribbean. Legislation restricting foreign equity and profit repatriation was widespread in the 1970s, as were protests against discriminatory U.S. commercial legislation. By the end of the 1970s, less than 33 percent of Latin America's exports went to the U.S. market, down from 50 percent two decades earlier.

The rise of nationalism and revolution in Latin America reflected the general destabilization of the economic, social, and political structures of the region. The region's economy was also affected by an agrarian crisis, the exhaustion of import substitution industrialization, and the world economic recession. The first reduced peasant earnings below subsistence levels, causing migration to overcrowded cities where enormous belts of misery proliferated conspicuously, providing fertile ground for revolutionary movements. The countryside surrounded the city in a new way.

New social classes engendered by partial modernization and industrialization sought political expression, which was frequently blocked by U.S.-backed political elites. Media sympathetic to the United States earned the suspicion of the influential younger generation of journalists, academics, and intellectuals now shaping public opinion, for whom best-sellers of the 1950s, like the Spanish-language version of *Readers' Digest,* were "CIA organs." Anti-Yankee sentiment became fashionable, along with a certain "satanization" of the United States.

Latin American governments responded to these pressures, and U.S. political influence declined. In the 1970s Latin American countries united behind Panama, demanded reforms in the OAS, spurned the Inter-American Treaty of Reciprocal Assistance (the Rio Treaty of 1947), lifted the embargo against Cuba, voted for the PRC's entrance into the United Nations, and supported Arab positions against Israel. How far Latin America had moved from the old days was demonstrated in 1980 by its widespread ignoring of the U.S. Olympic games boycott.

In the 1970s the saturation of the home markets in the partially industrialized Latin American countries led to their efforts to increase exports—now of light manufactured goods—at a time when markets were shrinking and protectionism was rising in the developed countries. Impelled by this need to find new outlets for its manufacturers and seeking to escape dependence on U.S. markets, capital, and technology, Latin American countries began to pursue broader economic relations with the outside world. Regional trade doubled between the early 1950s and the late 1970s, and regional economic organizations proliferated. Latin American countries joined other Third World countries in more than a dozen raw material producers' organizations and took a leading role in the North-South dialogue and in the economic commissions and conferences of the United Nations. Western Europe came to rival the United States as the region's leading trading partner as West European and Japanese equity came to surpass that of the United States in major countries like Argentina and Brazil.

Political contacts during this period also deepened with both the Third World and Western Europe. Latin American countries joined Third World nonaligned organizations and heads of state, and joint intergovernmental communiqué and delegations in international forums that resoundingly declared solidarity with the causes of Asia, Africa, and the Middle East. The international economic foundations and political organizations of the European Christian and Social Democratic parties established ties with Latin American trade unions, peasant organizations, and political parties.

This proliferation and expansion of external relations extended to the Soviet Union and the economic association of East European countries, the Council for Mutual Economic Assistance (CMEA). In 1964, the Soviet Union traded with only 4 Latin American countries; by 1975, the number had risen to 20. Soviet-Latin American trade increased 13.5 times between 1960 and 1977, making it "one of the most dynamic segments of the socialist countries' international trade."[2]

During the 1970s "a qualitatively new stage in developing Soviet-Latin American economic cooperation" began, a Soviet analyst announced in the first joint CMEA work on Latin America.[3] Most analysts in Latin America view this new relationship as a step in an emergence from U.S. tutelage and as a diversification in international relations—as complementary, even integral, to Latin America's new independence and antiimperialist vocation. Although this view is surely valid, and although there are tangible benefits in extending economic relations with the Soviet bloc, there is nevertheless another relevent context in which to view the changing relationship: Soviet global and regional strategy. The following chapters will examine this other dimension of Latin America's new relationship with the Soviet bloc.

2

Soviet Strategy
and the Third World

Latin America occupies a special place in the "third world" which not long ago was determined in particular by its separation from the world socialist system. That situation is changing. In the struggle for the strengthening of national sovereignty, for economic development and for an independent foreign policy, the Latin American countries tend more and more to develop relations with the Soviet Union and with other states of the socialist community.[4]

According to myriad Soviet declarations, the Soviet Union not only "advances and defends the sovereignty and independence of the Latin American countries against the encroachment of imperialism" but "*only* cooperation with socialist countries . . . can accelerate the economic and social development of the young states."[5] (Author's italics.) Are relations with the Soviet bloc indispensable to overcoming Latin America's dependency or are they part of a new threat to Latin American independence? A brief review of the general economic experience of the Third World begins to answer this question.

According to Soviet spokesmen, "Multiform collaboration with 'third world' countries for the sake of strengthening their economic independence and elevating the living standards of their peoples is the principal line pursued by the socialist states."[6] Moscow claims to be the natural ally of the developing countries and to share their fundamental interests. Soviet policy statements reject any "responsibility for the economic backwardness which the developing countries inherited from the colonial past" because socialist states "never pursued and do not pursue the economic exploitation of any countries whatsoever." This is because in these countries, unlike the West, there are "no parasitic classes making profits and superprofits" from other countries.[7]

According to these same spokesmen, "Developing countries are convinced by their own experience that their economic co-operation with socialist countries promotes their social progress and the prosperity of their peoples."[8] Yet strangely enough, at international conferences the Soviet Union has come under increasing fire from Third World countries. At the fourth United Nations Conference on Trade and Development (UNCTAD IV) in May 1976 one delegate after another rose to denounce Soviet economic practices in the Third World. A Bolivian delegate remarked, "We're madder at the Soviet Union and its friends than even at the West." An African delegate expatiated at length on the inequities of Soviet-Third World trade, and "many delegates murmured agreement" with China's accusation of the Soviets' "criminal exploitation of the Third World." A Yugoslav commented, "There's no question about it, the USSR is not popular here."[9] Indeed, experience has convinced Third World countries to be skeptical about Soviet claims.

Economic Strings

In fact, Soviet economic performance in the Third World
has been no better, probably far worse, and certainly more
hypocritical, than that of the West. Moscow attacks world
market prices as "one of the methods by which monopolists
take a large part of the developing countries' national income through unequal exchange,"[10] but prices in Soviet foreign trade are governed by those on the world market.[11] The
Soviets have regularly obligated their Third World trading
partners to pay prices well above those of the world
market.[12] The same discrepancy between words and deeds
recurs in currency relations, where the Soviets loudly extol
the benefits of their bilateral trade, purportedly based on local currencies and barter. In actual contracts, however,
they prudently inject clauses guaranteeing themselves all
the advantages of the considerable undervaluation of Third
World currencies, thrusting the burden of devaluations on
to their trading partners.

The composition of Soviet-Third World trade is similar
to that of the West and "remains firmly within an 'imperialist' pattern."[13] In 1976, according to Soviet statistics, ap-
proximately 85 percent of Soviet imports from Third World
countries were raw materials and foodstuffs, while most of
the rest were light and semimanufactured products.[14] On
the other hand, nearly 75 percent of Soviet exports to these
countries were industrial goods (more than 50 percent
arms).[15]

The interest rates on Soviet credit to the Third World
have been marginally lower than for Western aid and a few
points below rates on regular international loans, but grace
and maturity periods are far shorter, rescheduling is much
more difficult, discounts smaller, and technical assistance
fees are charged.[16] By the mid-1970s, major recipients of So-

viet aid were paying as much or more to service their debt than they were receiving.[17] Virtually all Soviet aid is tied to purchases of inferior Soviet equipment, which is priced 10–20 percent above world prices.[18] Soviet planning bodies evaluate aid proposals on a profitmaking basis, signaling the conversion of the Soviet Union into what Lenin in his *Imperialism: the Highest Stage of Capitalism* called a "rentier state." As one Soviet economist has stated, "it is well known . . . that the Soviet Union has long since itself become a major international creditor."[19] Or, as another puts it, "to the USSR granting credits and other aid to the backward nations is not a charitable undertaking but assistance on a commercial basis."[20] Although the commercial criteria easily preempt international duty in Soviet calculations, even these yield to higher concerns: Soviet geopolitical goals. Two-thirds of Soviet aid and over half of Soviet sales to the Third World are military. (Such are the conditions of the arms race that most weapons become obsolete before being fired, but Third World countries provide an ideal market for obsolete arms.) Although Soviet-Third World military sales meet commercial criteria, their primary motive is the securing of a foothold in strategically located Third World countries.

Soviet military assistance creates dependency: for spare parts, ammunition, replacement equipment, and technical advisers for operation and maintenance. For both civil and military technical assistance the Soviets insist on the appointment of their own agencies as technical consultants and for all feasibility studies, detailed reports, drawings, and designs. These policies result not only in technological dependence on the Soviet Union and the stunting of the recipient's technological capacity, but also on continually increasing numbers of Soviet technicians, the training of Third World students in the Soviet Union, and, as a result, the creation of a Soviet-oriented scientific and technological elite.

Military assistance is generally part of a coordinated aid program involving the training of military personnel, the expansion of communications, the building of airfields, the development of commercial fishing, access to ports, and the obtaining of overflight rights. Advisers from Soviet bloc countries, in an increasingly evolved division of labor, are usually part of the package. The Soviets have found that such integrated programs provide a better method for creating a global infrastructure for Soviet military power.

The Soviet Offensive

Since 1965 the Soviet Union has carried out the greatest peacetime military buildup in history, which, overlapping a U.S. strategic retreat, has produced massive changes in the global military balance. The Soviet Union overtook the United States in most categories of strategic nuclear power and widened to a considerable margin its conventional force superiority. During these years the Soviet Union acquired the capacity to implement an offensive strategy with a global navy and an aerial attack force, enabling it to air and sealift troops and equipment over long distances and giving them a first-strike and counterforce nuclear capacity. These capabilities have been utilized to underwrite Soviet strategic deployment in the Third World, especially in the Indian Ocean and in Africa.

The expansion of Soviet commercial, political, and military relations with the Third World in the 1960s laid the groundwork for their strategic offensive in the 1970s. In the early 1960s Soviet vessels began oceanographic surveys of the entire Indian Ocean. The USSR soon was seeking footholds along the Indian Ocean littoral and on strategically important islands like the Seychelles. They signed Friendship Treaties, obtained access to bases, ports, moorings, and anchorages and used them to increase ship visits. The Soviets penetrated and sought to subvert national liberation movements. In Africa they set up military training programs or naval facilities in each of the three Guineas. On the nearby islands of the São Tome and Principe they obtained naval facilities as well. With Mauritania they signed a joint fishing agreement, a usual precursor to naval facilities. In Angola they nurtured an intimate relationship with the Popular Movement for the Liberation of Angola (MPLA). The Soviet Union's image as a "natural ally" of national liberation movements and its relations with Cuba, Vietnam, and several African, Asian, and Middle Eastern countries smoothed the path for a Soviet offensive in the Third World, which began in Angola in 1975.

The Soviets coordinated and equipped the air and sealift of 20 thousand Cuban troops into Angola in the late summer of 1975.[21] This was followed by attempted Soviet-backed coups in the Sudan and North Yemen and by a successful one in South Yemen. In 1977 the Soviets and Cubans intervened to save their Ethiopian client state from collapse with a massive airlift that injected more than a billion dollars worth of military equipment into the country in one month. After Angola and Ethiopia, Soviet strategists affirmed an enormous increase in Soviet bloc capability "for immediate intervention, particularly by means of rapidly moving large military units and armaments over large distances."[22]

In 1978 the Soviets backed an armed takeover in Afghanistan. That same year, hard on the heels of a military treaty with the Soviet Union, Vietnam occupied Kampuchea with the aid of several hundred million dollars worth of military hardware, air and sealifted by the Soviets. In

1979 the Soviets directly invaded Afghanistan, now occupied by more than 90 thousand Soviet troops. In 1980 Libya invaded Chad with Soviet arms and equipment. In the same year the Soviets acquired a permanent naval base in the Dahlak archipelago off the coast of Eritrea. This joined three other Soviet bases in South Yemen, constituting "a strategic pincer movement which could enable Moscow's forces to control access to the Red Sea."[23] While Third World resistance to Soviet expansionism grows and Moscow has suffered important reverses, most notably in Egypt, the gains easily outweigh the losses.

These advances constitute severe Soviet pressure on the raw material life lines of Western Europe and Japan. This is the central military component of a Soviet strategy designed to neutralize Europe and Japan. It accompanies military pressure on the flanks of NATO (such as the buildup on the Kola peninsula, persistent violations of Norwegian and Swedish neutrality, and the expansion of the Soviet Eastern Mediterranean fleet), the growth of Warsaw Pact forces, the elimination of the NATO theater nuclear deterrent, and the naval installations on Japan's Kurile islands. All this complements a sustained ideological, economic, political, and diplomatic campaign to encourage neutralist and pacifist sentiment in Western Europe and Japan aimed at weakening or severing the Western alliance.

The Soviet Union has employed a wide variety of instruments in pursuing its strategic objectives in the Third World. Along with trade, aid, and technical and military measures, political and cultural assistance has played a major role. Politically the Soviets have sought to identify themselves with Third World causes and to portray the United States as the main enemy of Third World countries. While party-to-party relations remain important, since the 1960s the USSR has urged local Communist parties to form alliances with the local middle class and the military.

Meanwhile, the Soviet Union has developed relations with governments, opposition movements, and political fronts deemed ripe for penetration. The sophisticated Soviet intelligence apparatus, sharpened by years of vigilance against its own citizens, has been employed in espionage, covert action, bribery, provocation, and disinformation campaigns. Cultural activities including the formation of Soviet "friendship societies," cultural, student, and sports exchanges, radio and television broadcasts, and film festivals and the like are utilized for information gathering, propaganda, and the formation of local lobbies.

In Latin America, too, the Soviets have pursued their objectives with majestic impartiality, using not only sympathetic parties and guerrilla organizations but also reform movements, military juntas, and even right-wing dictatorships. In the following chapters we shall examine the Soviet strategy for Latin America and the methods utilized to implement it.

3

The Peaceful Road to Sovietism

In the wake of the Soviet military buildup and the USSR's strategic deployment throughout the Third World, Soviet Latin American policy eventually shifted from a low-risk, peaceful penetration to a line favoring armed struggle in selected countries. In this chapter and the next we shall trace this shift and contemplate its implications.

Soviet Diplomatic Offensive

From the late 1950s to the late 1970s Soviet Latin American policy developed in the context of peaceful coexistence and détente. By the late 1950s the Soviet Union had acquired the ambitions of a superpower without the military capacity, the industrial base, or the overseas resources to rival the United States. Peaceful coexistence was a policy designed to shelter the Soviet Union from challenges to its spheres of influence, to reduce the possibility of distracting overseas adventures, to promote trade with the West for the acquisition of the technology to build a military industrial base, to stimulate trade with the Third World for needed raw materials, foodstuffs, and markets and for foreign exchange for purchases from the West. A broad expansion of diplomatic and commercial relations was required to implement the new policy. The endorsement of "the peaceful road to socialism" at the twentieth congress of the Soviet Communist Party in February of 1956 was a signal to Western and Third World governments that the Soviets were prepared to offer a policy of accommodation by local Communist parties in exchange for improved state-to-state relations. Peaceful coexistence and peaceful transition were inseparably linked in a Soviet strategy of accumulation of force.

The new line represented a reversal of Soviet Third World policy. Armed revolution was now discouraged in favor of "peaceful liberation from foreign oppression."[24] With the advent of nuclear weapons, local wars represented a threat to world peace, because even a tiny spark could cause a world conflagration."[25] The national liberation struggle had entered a new stage in which economic consolidation had become its central task and "the basic link in the further development of the revolution."[26] In this new stage the socialist system under Soviet leadership was to become the main force in the battle against imperialism.[27] Soviet success in peaceful competition with capitalism and its economic assistance would enable the emerging nations to "avoid the dangers of a new enslavement."[28] In years to come this theme would be repeated insistently: Third World independence was "altogether impossible without assistance from the socialist countries."[29] The traditional Leninist *alliance* of socialism and national liberation was transformed into Third World *reliance* on the Soviet Union.

After Leonid Brezhnev came to power in the Soviet Union in October 1964, peaceful liberation was seasoned with a measure of selective rhetorical support for wars of national liberation under pressure from Vietnam, Cuba, North

Korea, and others in accordance with the Soviet assessment of the declining U.S. global position. Nonetheless, aside from Vietnam and, much later, other selected countries in "the national liberation zone," peaceful coexistence and peaceful transition prevailed. In most of the Third World this policy provided cooperative Communist parties in exchange for Soviet access to local elites and to diplomatic and commercial relations with Third World governments.

In Latin America after 1960 the Soviet Union opposed Cuban-sponsored guerrilla movements, encouraged local Communist parties to join broad electoral fronts, and persistently sought diplomatic and commercial relations with established governments. At the beginning of the 1960s the Soviet Union enjoyed diplomatic relations with only three Latin American countries (Argentina, Mexico, and Uruguay). After Fidel Castro's revolution in Cuba in January of 1959 Moscow launched a full-scale campaign to establish diplomatic relations with the other Latin American nations.

The harvest was meager at first. U.S. opposition to Soviet backing for Castro slowed progress; initially only Cuba (1960), Brazil (1961), and Chile (1964) accepted Soviet overtures. By the late 1960s, however, Latin American countries themselves began to expand their foreign relations, and détente diminished U.S. resistance. Colombia (1968), and Peru, Ecuador, and Bolivia (1969) established ties with the Soviet Union and were joined later by Venezuela and Guyana in 1970. By 1970 the presence of some 300 Soviet diplomatic personnel and large Soviet diplomatic, economic, cultural, and scientific missions throughout Latin America had significantly expanded Soviet contacts with governments and with the social, economic, and political elites.[30] During the early 1970s diplomatic ties were established with Costa Rica, Trinidad and Tobago, Guatemala, Nicaragua, and Jamaica. At this time a Soviet propagandist boasted that "the invisible wall behind which the USA has been keeping Latin America from the socialist world has virtually collapsed."[31] By the end of the 1970s the Soviet Union had established diplomatic relations with 19 Latin American countries.

Soviet Commercial Offensive

Diplomatic relations were frequently preceded by commercial relations, though the latter usually remained at a low level until diplomatic ties were formed. Although subject to wide fluctuations, trade between Latin America and the Soviet Union climbed from $70 million in 1960 to $912 million in 1979 (and was well over a billion dollars in 1980 according to preliminary figures). (See Table 1.) By 1979 the Soviet Union traded with ten Latin American countries, up from four in 1960, but the bulk of its Latin American commerce concentrated in Argentina and Brazil.[32] These two countries absorbed 60 percent of total Soviet exports to Latin America in 1979, down from 94 percent in 1960. In the mid-1970s, Peru, Bolivia, Colombia, and Panama became major Soviet markets.[33]

Soviet exports to Latin America mainly include tractors, automobiles, trolleys, buses, machine tools, hydroelectric and thermal turbines, and, in the case of Peru, military equipment. Soviet purchases from Latin America consist mainly of raw materials and foodstuffs. Purchases from Argentina include wool yarn, grain, meat, and wine; from Brazil, coffee, cocoa, rice, wool, and clothing; from Peru, nonferrous metals, fish meal, coffee, and wool; and from Bolivia, tin.[34] The acquisition of cheap Latin American raw materials and foodstuffs, sometimes but not always in exchange for Soviet bloc industrial equipment, became the cornerstone of Soviet bloc-Latin American trade.

Soviet bloc credits to Latin America (not including

TABLE 1
Soviet Trade with Latin America (Excluding Cuba)
(in U.S. $ Millions)

	Exports	Imports	Turnover
1960 (5 years)	31.9	36.2	68.1
1965 ,,	49.7	108.7	158.5
1970	8.7	78.0	86.7
1971	15.9	123.5	139.4
1972	31.5	140.6	172.1
1973	49.0	299.9	348.9
1974	148.9	405.3	554.2
1975	190.6	970.8	1161.4
1976	150.7	866.4	1017.1
1977	229.9	682.7	912.6

Source: *United Nations Commission on Trade and Development,* UNC-TAD V, TD/243, Supplement 2, p. 18 (Table 3), based on Soviet national foreign trade handbooks.

Cuba) rose rapidly in the late 1960s and early 1970s. (See Table 2.) In 1968 the region received only 0.5 percent of total Soviet bloc credits to the less developed countries (LDCs). This rose to 30 percent by 1973, and in the late 1970s was still about 15 percent. In the late 1960s Soviet Union credits to Latin America rose slowly, but by 1972 they had climbed 130 percent above 1969. By the end of 1974, Soviet bloc credit offers were nearly $2 billion.[35] In 1974 Argentina received more Soviet bloc credits than any other LDC.[36] Peru followed Argentina in CMEA credit disbursements to Latin America between 1970 and 1976, receiving a total of $228 million.[37]

Until the late 1960s, the absence of Soviet economic missions in Latin America meant that trade was carried out

TABLE 2
CMEA Trade with Latin America (Including Cuba)
(in U.S. $ Millions)

	Year						Annual Average Growth Rate		Percentage Rate of Change Over Previous Year		
	1960	1965	1970	1975	1976	1977	1960–1965	1965–1970	1970–1975	1976	1977
Exports	242	584	933	2407	2745	3383	19.3	9.8	21.0	14.0	23.2
% of total to LDCs	21.4%	21.0%	19.6%	19.4%	20.5%	19.9%					
Imports	279	766	993	3763	4102	4560	22.5	5.3	30.0	9.0	11.1
% of total from LDCs	21.8%	31.4%	28.4%	33.0%	34.8%	34.2%					
Turnover	521	1350	1926	6170	6847	7943	21.0	7.4	26.0	11.0	16.0
% of total LDCs	21.6%	25.9%	23.4%	26.0%	27.2%	26.2%					

Source: United Nations Commission on Trade and Development, UNCTAD V, TD/243, Supplement 2 (Table 2), based on national trade statistics.

20

mainly through intermediaries. But from that time on the Soviet Union and other CMEA countries signed numerous industrial and commercial accords, most-favored nation treaties, long-term raw material delivery contracts, and technical and scientific aid agreements. The USSR energetically sought the formation of intergovernmental commissions headed by senior economic policymakers at the ministerial level to coordinate all aspects of economic intercourse.[38]

This institutionalization of economic relations has been accompanied by frequent visits by heads of state and representatives of business circles and by increased participation in fairs and expositions. Beginning in 1975, the CMEA and individual Latin American countries concluded multilateral economic agreements. Latin American economic organizations—the Latin American Economic System (SELA), for example—have also signed accords with the CMEA, which Cuba has joined outright and in which other Latin American countries such as Mexico and Guyana participate as observers. In this way Moscow has forged, in the words of one Soviet analyst, "an integral system of commercial, economic, and technico-scientific collaboration."[39]

Scientific and technical collaboration has been pursued largely through universities in the form of training of professionals and specialists, joint studies between the Soviet and Latin American governments, and the granting of scholarships for study in the USSR and Eastern Europe. Between 1956 and 1973 an estimated 6,290 Latin American students studied in Soviet bloc countries; in 1970 2,425 students were attending Soviet bloc academic institutions.[40] Soviet oceanographic vessels began to chart the seas surrounding Latin America in the late 1960s and the Soviet merchant marine and fishing fleet could be found in Latin American ports. Reciprocal visits by business, professional, trade union, military, and youth groups multiplied, as did governmental and parliamentary delegations. By 1967, parliamentary delegations from Uruguay, Bolivia, Mexico,

Chile, Peru, Venezuela, Colombia, and Costa Rica had already visited the Soviet Union, and delegations from the Supreme Soviet had visited Mexico, Bolivia, and Chile.[41] From 1967 to 1972 there was an enormous increase in film festivals, cultural expositions, Soviet Spanish-language book publishing, and radio broadcasting for Latin America.[42]

Propaganda activities in Latin America during this period tried to direct rising Latin American nationalism against the United States. Consistent with USSR diplomatic and commercial overtures to established Latin American governments, Soviet intentions were not to install pro-Soviet regimes or to acquire Soviet bases in the hemisphere, but rather to undermine U.S. positions there. Soviet authorities characterized Latin America as the U.S. "strategic rear" and published studies detailing U.S. dependence on Latin America for raw materials, especially strategic raw materials, and particularly "new types of raw materials used in missile, commmunication and atomic industries."[43] Their studies also analyzed the Inter-American defense system, maritime navigation, and continental and oceanic geology and topography. The Soviets geared their studies and policies for a future challenge to U.S. hegemony.

Opposition from Cuba

Soviet policy in Latin America was a major source of friction with Fidel Castro, who enjoyed a considerable degree of independence in this period. Although Castro also saw U.S. imperialism as the main enemy, he bitterly resented the practice of "socialist governments that give aid to Latin American oligarchs" and "hamper the work of true revolutionaries," the guerrillas.[44]

The policy of peaceful transition was pursued with singular dedication in Latin America. Opposition to it from Cuba (along with China, Albania, Vietnam, and North Korea) led to splits in many Latin American Communist parties in the 1960s. The supporters of the Soviet policy generally retained control of the official party apparatus and received unstinting support from the USSR, which urged them to concentrate on organizing urban workers, professionals, academics, and government officials and to join with the reformist opposition in broad electoral coalitions. In Chile, for example, the solidly pro-Soviet Chilean Communist Party, after its defeat in the 1964 elections in coalition with the Socialist Party, backed the Christian Democratic victor Eduardo Frei, to the disgust of the Cubans.

Castroite groupings arose in the early 1960s to oppose the traditional Communist parties and the Soviet line. The Soviets reproached these "new vanguards" who questioned "the leading role of the working class and of its party" and sought to put in its place "political-military fronts."[45] Yet, in replying to the Fidelistas' accusations of reformism, opportunism, and conciliationism, the Soviets and their sympathizers were usually quite restrained. Although excoriating their political views, the Soviets were careful not to read out of the movement forces they were seeking eventually to harness. Pro-Soviets like Luis Corvalan, secretary general of the Chilean Communist Party, labeled the Castroites "petty-bourgeois revolutionaries" who

> tend at times to underrate the workers and the Communist parties, to gravitate towards nationalism, recklessness, terror and, at times, even anti-communism and anti-Sovietism. . . . But they are revolutionary all the same, and the proletariat must put the accent on unity with them rather than on fighting their mistakes.[46]

In a similar vein Gregor Karstag, writing in the Soviet journal *Latinskaya Amerika,* explained

> The Latin American petit-bourgeois revolutionaries, understand [the Cuban] experience extremely one-sid-

edly and at the same time mechanically transfer it to the other countries of Latin America. . . . The notions of "guerrilla strategy," while reflecting in a distorted manner the positive fact of attracting broader and broader masses into the revolutionary struggle . . ., are the views of petit-bourgeois revolutionaries who are voluntaristically trying to fit reality to their theory.[47]

For the Soviets, the fundamental deviation of the Castroites was their refusal to allow "objective conditions" to ripen, becoming "impatient" and "running forward from reality." Their evasion of even "a minimal calculation of the concrete conditions and the actual correlation of forces" doomed them to "certain destruction."[48]

The Castroite groups boycotted the broad united fronts called for by the traditional Communist parties. The pro-Cuban Revolutionary Left Movement (MIR) stayed out of the Popular Unity front in Chile, and the Peruvian MIR, the Tupamaros in Uruguay, and other Castroite groups in Bolivia, Colombia, El Salvador, Guatemala, and Venezuela pursued similar policies. Yet by the early 1970s the guerrilla groups had made little headway, where they had not been liquidated entirely, and the traditional Communist parties were participating with reformists and nationalists in apparently thriving united fronts in Bolivia, Chile, Ecuador, Peru, and Uruguay—while fostering others in such places as Venezuela, Argentina, Mexico, and Jamaica. The Conference of Central American and Mexican Communist Parties in June 1971 unanimously called for a "regional united front" with other opposition forces "to direct Latin American public opinion towards the struggle for achieving an independent economic and cultural development."[49]

The Popular Unity government in Chile, which took office as a result of the electoral victory of a broad coalition of Communist, Socialist, radical and leftist Christian forces in September 1970, was at once the crowning achievement and the downfall of the policy of peaceful transition to socialism. The Popular Unity victory received extraordinary attention at the twenty-fourth congress of the Soviet Communist Party in 1971, where it was hailed by Brezhnev and termed the vindication of the Soviet line of peaceful transition.[50] Indeed, the victory in Chile was considered "largely [sic] the result of the solidarity between the working class of the Latin American countries and the moral support of the socialist countries."[51] This, according to the congress, was the view of "the Chilean comrades themselves."[52] According to a leading Soviet authority on Latin America the Chilean victory was

> but evidence of the radical change in the world correlation of forces. The power, the influence and the prestige of socialism in the international arena have reached such a dimension that even the ingenious apparatus of bourgeois democracy . . . could not prevent the most advanced sector of the people . . . from forming a constitutional government based on marxist-leninist ideas. . . . In Chile due to new international conditions the possibility emerged to pass to socialism the peaceful way.[53]

The success of peaceful transition in Chile was offered as an example "to the peoples of Latin America . . . of bold progress toward liberation from the oppression of American imperialism," and "after Cuba, another freedom torch" illuminating the entrance to a "new stage" in the Latin American revolution.[54] Clearly, Chile was to be only the first fruit of the Soviet policy.

The Peaceful Road and the Military Coup

Beyond Chile the twenty-fourth congress saw bright prospects in "the new type of officers who are progressive nationalists" and who were "rapidly strenghtening their interest in a number of Latin American countries,"[55] a phenomenon expected to "accelerate the course of revolutionary developments."[56] In the late 1960s and early 1970s military coups in Panama, Ecuador, Bolivia, and Peru brought to power populist regimes reminiscent of those of Lazaro Cardenas's Mexico and Getulio Vargas's Brazil in the 1930s and Juan Peron's Argentina in the 1940s. The new military governments promulgated extensive social reforms, nationalized the property of U.S. multinationals, and often welcomed Soviet diplomatic and economic overtures. Taken together with the victory of Chile's Popular Unity front, the advance of the Broad Front in Uruguay, and Peron's return to Argentina, these military governments signaled to the Soviets

> the upsurge of the revolutionary movement on the Latin American continent . . . of tremendous importance to the world revolutionary process. Seemingly quite reliable rear lines of American imperialism are becoming a tremendous hotbed of anti-imperialist revolution. A tremendously powerful revolutionary movement is developing by the side of the main citadel of imperialism, the U.S. These changes are having and, unquestionably, will continue to have, a strong impact on the further changes in the correlation of world forces in favor of the international working class and socialism.[57]

The Soviets paid special attention to the "new state forms . . . characterized by the participation of the armed forces in progressive developments."[58] Soviet analysts believed that the modernization of Latin American armies had given rise to a new generation of military officers from "the petty-bourgeois stratum of the population which reacts extremely sensitively and sharply to social problems."[59] Among these patriotically-inclined officers there had emerged "a radical anti-imperialist trend, brought about by their awareness of the fact that under conditions of imperialist dependence it is impossible to achieve national progress."[60] Moreover, "among the military . . . there are groups which do not conceal their admiration for the Soviet Union."[61] This acknowledgement of Soviet sympathizers among the local officer corps was accompanied by intensive efforts to foster pro-Soviet factions in the Latin American military.

According to Soviet authorities, the new trends among Latin American military personnel were brought about "most of all by the change in the interrelationship of forces in the world" and espcially "by the increasing might of the Soviet state and of the entire socialist system."[62] Moscow's appropriation of the gains of Latin American nationalism corresponded to a previously noted shift in Soviet self-advertisements. No longer content to be the supporter of Third World liberation, it had become its executor. Similarly, the ever more explicit criterion for the title of progressive and anti-imperialist had become the extent of a regime's friendship with the Soviet Union and its hostility toward the United States.

Although opposition to the United States and receptivity to the Soviet Union were sufficient credentials to qualify regimes as progressive, the Soviets endeavored to resolve the contradiction between their sponsorship of popular revolution and broad democratic fronts and their support for military regimes that suppressed revolutionary groups and curtailed opposition activities. In the revised Soviet assessment, the armed forces were "the sole stable institution in a general background of chronic political instability in the political life of Latin America" characterized by "an abundance of corrupt bourgeois parties, continually fighting among themselves and not enjoying the support of the people."[63] In such conditions the military "may fulfill a role as an ally of the progessive forces."[64] All the more because "the form of revolutionary development . . . largely depends on the position adopted by the army."[65] At this time Salvador Allende's victory in Chile was described as a reaffirmation of this conclusion as "the neutral attitude of the army was one of the major factors governing the victory of the Popular Unity Bloc."[66] Because the armed road to power had been based on the need "to smash the bourgeois state machine" and, above all, the army, the willingness of the army to permit or even to sponsor progressive developments removed the necessity for armed struggle.[67] In this fashion military coups were reconciled with the peaceful transition to socialism, and it was now clear that socialism had come to mean "sovietism." For some Latin American socialists and nationalists it was becoming evident that peaceful transition was not a strategy for socialism at all but for aligning these countries with the Soviet Union.

The September 1973 coup in Chile dashed the high hopes for a relatively peaceful transition to a Soviet alignment and delivered a telling blow to the Soviet line worldwide. Early Soviet commentators sought to deflect criticism that would call into question the basic party line and instead blamed the Castroite MIR and other "ultra left" groups. Nonetheless seeds of doubt which were to bear fruit in the late 1970s had been planted in the minds of Soviet analysts. Even at this time Soviet authorities agreed that the preservation of links between the Chilean military and the United States had been fatal.

It is probable that one of the motives behind the Soviets' generous provisions of sophisticated military equipment and technical assistance to Peru in 1973 was to weaken the links between the Peruvian military and the Pentagon. After Augusto Pinochet's coup in Chile, Peru became the main recipient of Soviet economic and military assistance in Latin America after Cuba.[68]

With the ascension of General Morales Bermudez in

1975, the Peruvian military government reopened the door to heavy U.S. investment. In addition to this, the coup in Chile, right-wing takeovers in Bolivia and Uruguay, and the toppling of the Peronist government in Argentina prompted many noted Soviet Latin America specialists and local Communist party leaders to lament that their previous proclamations about a revolutionary upheaval in the region had been widely off the mark. G. Mirskii, hitherto one of the most outspoken enthusiasts for the "patriotic military," noted that the progressive spirit of the military "reached its limit," and exclaimed that a "reactionary counteroffensive . . . unprecedented in Latin American history" was "swallowing up one country after another."[69]

This despondency was not shared by Kremlin leaders, for whom ideology had long taken a back seat to global strategic considerations. What appeared to certain academicians as a disastrous setback in the revolutionary process was but an indication to the Soviet leadership that a further refining of tactics was in order. Throughout Europe and the Western Hemisphere Soviet propagandists concentrated their fire on the atrocities of Pinochet's Chile—the symbol of U.S. imperialism's revanchism, yet the period of "reactionary counteroffensive" in South America after 1973 was one in which Moscow stepped up its economic relations with Bolivia, furnished arms to Peru on an unprecedented scale, and waged a vigorous campaign to win over the Argentine military with increased trade and credit and multiple military missions, while blocking discussions of Argentine human rights violations in the United Nations.

Soviet appreciation of military regimes in South America was now entirely divorced from any consideration of their progressiveness. Soviet friendship with Argentina became the cornerstone of its southern cone policy. That regime's only claim to progressiveness rested on its booming trade with the Soviet Union, its toleration of the pro-Soviet

Communist party (while proscribing all other leftist groups), and its hostility to Chile, whom the Soviets were seeking to isolate. Nonetheless, on this basis, the Soviets and their Argentine followers drew elaborate distinctions between the progressive forces in the Argentine military and the "pinochetistas" (that is, the anti-Soviets).[70] According to Argentine Communist Party leaders, the latter were but "one current in the Argentine government, a minority."[71] The Argentine Communist Party supported President General Jorge Videla's proposals to put the country "on a broad democratic basis,"[72] That government, which was violating human rights more widely than even Pinochet's Chile, was the hope for an evolution "on a clearly progressive basis," while the enemy represented the "ultrareactionary intrigues" of "Pinochetism."[73] The motive for Moscow's fine discriminations among military regimes clearly had little to do with progressiveness or with the peaceful transition to socialism and everything to do with efforts to gain a Soviet beachhead in South America.

4

The Soviet Strategic Offensive in Latin America

In 1979, armed struggle became the cardinal point of Soviet Latin American doctrine. The revolution in Nicaragua was the occasion for this shift, but Soviet support for armed struggle was not confined to one country. There was a general reversal of tactics, expressly applied to a growing number of Latin American countries and endorsed by the local Communist parties. In the wake of the Soviet military buildup and their strategic deployment in other parts of the Third World, this shift represented the Latin American echo of the Soviet global offensive. As with the peaceful transition to socialism, the new policy line for Latin America was part of a general revision—one already implemented in Africa, Asia, and the Middle East well before the outbreak of revolution in Central America provided conditions suitable for its application to Latin America.

In 1977 Karen Brutents, a member of the Central Committee of the Soviet Communist Party and a leading specialist on the Third World, enunciated the changed Soviet strategic posture. In the past this was largely a matter of defense of the first socialist revolution against imperialism, whereas today it is a question of carrying on the offensive against imperialism and world capitalism as a whole in order to do away with them.[74]

Beginning in 1975, the Soviet Union backed armed coups, assassinations, invasions, occupations, and guerrilla movements in Angola, South Yemen, Sudan, Ethiopia, Kampuchea, Laos, Zaire, Afghanistan, and elsewhere. The net result gave substance to the claims of Brutents and others of a "changed correlation of forces on a world scale." Correspondingly, Soviet economic ties with the Third World, previously termed the main factor for Third World liberation, were downgraded in favor of military assistance. In the mid-1970s Soviet writers began to assert that under the new international conditions "material aid on the part of the socialist states has ceased to be a factor directly promoting the transition to a non-capitalist path" and that, instead, "the main factors, favoring such an orientation, are the political, military-strategic and moral influence of the states of the socialist community."[75] In Asia, Africa, and the Middle East, the Soviets once again became partisans of the armed road to power, but in an altered international context.

Crucial to Soviet success in Africa was the deployment of Cuban troops trained, equipped, and supported logistically by the Soviet Union. As we shall see in the next chapter, this could occur because, between 1968 and 1975, Cuba was economically and politically subjugated by the Soviet superpower. In these years Castro, under extreme Soviet pressure, gradually abandoned his opposition to Soviet peaceful transition and united fronts and adopted the domestic and international policies advocated by the Soviet Union. In the same years the Soviets modernized Cuba's military capacity and established a naval presence in the Caribbean.

Changed Soviet Policy

A favorable correlation of forces, proven successes in its new Third World strategy, and a compliant and well-fortified Cuba were factors that weighed heavily in the dramatic modification of Soviet Latin American policy at the end of the decade. Nonetheless, no such shift could have come about without compatible conditions within Latin America. A global strategy such as the Soviets pursue should not be thought of as a timetable or "hit list" enumerating governments to be overthrown by revolutions prefabricated in Moscow. Soviet strategic planning by no means precludes tactical flexibility, and the previous chapter amply demonstrates the Soviet capacity to tailor their policies to specific and changing realities. Even though Central American revolutions are autonomous, they certainly have presented the Soviet Union with a golden opportunity for advancing its objectives in the region.

Before the Nicaraguan revolution in 1979, Soviet analysts detected no such "upsurge of the revolutionary movement" as they had foreseen a decade before for the southern cone. This did not mean that the Cubans, who enjoy a certain degree of branch autonomy in this field, were not aware of, and indeed involved in, events in Nicaragua, or that they did not inform Moscow. But it is probably true that "only in 1978 did the Soviets and Cubans begin reassessing the chances for a successful revolution"[76] and that, until that time, as one Soviet analyst affirms, "none of us would utter an optimistic phrase about the future of that struggle."[77]

If the Nicaraguan revolution attracted little Soviet attention before it triumphed, it certainly received a great deal afterward. Not only did the Soviets move quickly to establish state-to-state and party-to-party relations with the new Sandinista regime, they carried out a thorough reevaluation of past doctrines and approaches in the light of the revolution's success. In his summary in an early 1980 symposium in *Latinskaya Amerika*, Sergo Mikoyan, editor in chief of the publication, declared that the Nicaraguan revolution was of "colossal international importance . . . one of those events that demand reexamination of established conceptions and their sacrifice."[78] As another contributor affirmed,

> The Nicaraguan experience demolished the previous simplistic interpretation of guerrilla actions, confirmed the justice of many of Che Guevara's strategic principles and crystallized his idea of creating a powerful popular guerrilla movement.[79]

The discussions of the Sandinista revolution marked the final relinquishment of peaceful transition in favor of armed struggle. Another contributor to the *Latinskaya Amerika* discussion asserted that the Nicaraguan revolution was living proof that "the armed road . . . is the most promising in the specific conditions of most of the Latin American countries."[80] Mikoyan then asserted that "there is not a single example of victorious revolution in the continent that has pursued the peaceful road" and that "only the armed road has led to victory in Latin America."[81] Six months later a definitive Soviet analysis of Chile completely reversed the earlier position by declaring categorically that by 1973 "the conditions for the peaceful transition to socialism no longer existed" and that the revolutionary movement had "failed to arm the people."[82]

Local Latin American Communist parties have also adopted the revised Soviet line. Chilean Communist Party leader Luis Corvalan, veteran exponent of the peaceful transition line, called for armed struggle in a speech to the second congress of the Cuban Communist Party in Havana in December 1980.[83] This was preceded by a speech in Moscow in

September in which Corvalan acknowledged the necessity of "acute violence" in Chile and pointed to Cuba and Nicaragua as precedents.[84] Rodney Arismendi, first secretary of the Uruguayan Communist Party and an influential theoretician, has also recently vindicated "guerrilla warfare as a method."[85] Central American Communist party leaders, even the leadership of the Costa Rican party, long accustomed to political democracy and peaceful political competition, have endorsed this policy shift unanimously.[86] Shafik Jorge Handel, leader of the Salvadoran party, writing in the Soviet Communist Party's theoretical organ *Kommunist*, declared that the revolutionary movement in El Salvador "will be victorious by the armed road . . . there is no other way."[87]

These shifts in the political line accompany changes in practical policy. In the spring of 1978, Nicaragua's traditional pro-Soviet party, the Nicaraguan Socialist Party, formed the People's Military Organization to coordinate military activities with the Sandinista National Liberation Front (FSLN).[88] In December 1979 the party in El Salvador agreed to set up a revolutionary coordinating body, (along with two armed guerrilla organizations), which was later expanded to five groups. In June of 1981 the Chilean Communist Party and the MIR issued a joint communiqué announcing the coordination of organizational bodies and assignments. Coordination or integration with organizations pursuing armed struggle, formerly scorned as "petty-bourgeois" and "ultra left," is now the order of the day for Communist parties in several other Latin American countries, including Guatemala, Colombia, Ecuador, and Costa Rica. Unlike the Cuban revolution itself, the Nicaraguan revolution, in a very different international environment, has produced, or rather occasioned, a general revision of Soviet positions with respect to the major tenets and the organizational embodiments of Castroism.

The Rehabilitation of Che Guevara

Latin American revolutionary leader Che Guevara, the bête noire in the 1960s of both the Soviets and the local Communist parties, has recently been rehabilitated in Soviet literature along with his main tactical principles. Guevara's belief that "it is not always necessary to wait until all the conditions are ripe for revolution; the *foco* [the guerrillas] can create them" heretofore condemned as "putschist," as "running forward from reality" and so forth, is now "lauded as a fundamental contribution to Latin American revolutionary movements."[89] Guevara's and Raul Castro's "little motor" of guerrilla actions that would ignite the "big motor" of popular insurrection has now, according to Mikoyan, "come into play . . . after 20 years of failure," a view echoed by the leaders of Latin American Communist parties.[90] Similarly, the Castroite political-military front, formerly regarded as the petty-bourgeois liquidation of the party, is now considered "capable in certain conditions of substituting as revolutionary vanguard for the political parties of the proletariat."[91]

These organizations and their tactics are no longer branded ultra left. It now appears that for a decade and a half there was confusion about this term, which should only be applied to "pseudorevolutionaries" and "demagogues" but not to "radical left revolutionaries."[92] Not only should there be an end to this abuse of the Castroites, not only should they now be praised, they should be joined. Kiva Maidanik, a prominent Latin American specialist at the Moscow Institute of World Economy and International Relations, maintains that "unity of the left, especially unity of the communist parties with those insurrectional forces which for decades have been branded 'ultraleft' " has become "the main the decisive link for pulling the revolution process forward."[93]

As early as the spring of 1979, before the Nicaraguan

revolution, Moscow was calling for "a regrouping of the ranks of the leftist forces of the continent."[94] In analyzing the Sandinista triumph, another Soviet specialist pointed to the unity of the revolutionary forces as a necessary condition for final victory.[95] This theme of left unity which "applies, first and foremost, to unity of the communist parties with insurgent movements, with left wing radical trends . . .," has been echoed by one local Communist party after another.[96] Antonio Castro of the Central Committee and the Political Commission of the Guatemalan Communist Party states that "the unity of the revolutionary forces is the key factor."[97] At the 13th congress of the pro-Soviet Popular Vanguard Party of Costa Rica, a special call was made for "strengthening unity with other parties which have adopted Marxism-Leninism as their doctrine."[98] The Ecuadoran Communist Party, like the Chilean and Salvadoran, has formed a broad front with other Left groups including the Castroites.[99]

Whereas today the USSR accepts and even recommends the dissolution of the party within a political-military front, a decade ago Soviet spokesmen held that self-sufficient Communist parties were "the decisive condition" for the creation of united fronts and that the dissolution of Communist parties or even ideological concessions on their part "would hinder the formation of united fronts."[100] If the Soviets are now advocating unity with Castroism, it is not because they have been bested in a debate on revolutionary tactics. As we shall describe in the next chapter, Castro succumbed a decade earlier to Soviet pressures and capitulated on every major ideological, political, and economic question.

The new Soviet advocacy of a "political-military front" is a consequence of "the changed correlation for forces on a global scale" and of their confidence in the bonds of dependency that tie Cuba to them. For several years the Soviets have been supporting political-military fronts in

Africa. Notable examples are Angola, Mozambique, Algeria, the Congo, and Zimbabwe. Within the Angolan MPLA, as in other similar groupings, they have promoted pro-Soviet factions to a leadership role. To such political-military fronts the Soviets portray Cuba as an example to be imitated.[101] From being the main opponent of the Soviet line, Cuba has become its main exponent and a model of pro-Soviet political development. If in a purely Latin American context the Soviet adoption of the repudiated Castroite line of the 1960s appears a revolution in strategy, in the context of the Soviet global offensive it signifies merely the belated application to Latin America of the new stage in Soviet strategy.

The "Socialist Orientation" of Latin America

A notable signal that Latin America has come within range of the Soviet global offensive is the recent inclusion in Soviet literature of Central America as a region in which states of "socialist orientation" are emerging.[102] Socialist orientation has become the new Soviet term for those developing countries aligning themselves with the Soviet Union.

In recent years Soviet leaders have elaborated with increasing precision the characteristics of a socialist orientation. Outstanding among them are "a revolutionary party guiding society and acting on the basis of scientific socialism," and "ties with the socialist countries,"[103] including "the establishment and development of multi-lateral cooperation with socialist states."[104] On reviewing the list of socialist oriented countries, it is evident that socialist orientation means Soviet orientation.

Until 1980 the Soviets designated only Africa and Asia as regions where socialist-oriented states were emerging. But in November 1980, Boris Ponomarev, the leading Soviet Central Committee authority on the Third World, explicitly included Central America.[105] Two months later Ponomarev wrote

> In the front ranks of the struggle are the states taking a socialist orientation. . . . On the whole, this relates to states in Asia, Africa and Central America which . . . are taking the road of transition to socialism.[106]

In contrast to the days of peaceful transition to socialism, the key element for the Soviets in socialist orientation is not economic ties with the Soviet Union but the dominance of pro-Soviet political forces. For other regions of the Third World,

> Moscow has accordingly evolved the notion of transforming existing political organizations into "vanguard parties." Soviet theoreticians over and over again emphasize that without such parties, socialist orientation cannot become true socialism.[107]

Here again for the Soviets Cuba is a classic example, but "comparable processes are taking place in Angola, Mozambique, the Congo, Algeria."[108] In 1976 the Soviet Communist Party and the Angolan MPLA signed an agreement calling for interparty cooperation and contact at all levels including systematic mutual consultation and cooperation in the training of cadres.[109] Similarly, the Soviets have urged the Sandinista FSLN to "create its own party and Sandinista mass organizations."[110] This, another Soviet writer explains, is "an essential condition for the organized strengthening of the Sandinista ranks . . . and for pursuing a uniform political course" and "to indoctrinate the Nicaraguans in a spirit of internationalism."[111] In March of 1980 a plan for ties between the Communist Party of the Soviet Union and the FSLN in 1980-1981 was signed.[112]

An emerging Soviet strategy in Central America is to procure states of socialist orientation by identifying and supporting armed revolutionary movements to obtain political and military leverage in the new governments. Sergo Mikoyan argues that the Chilean experience demonstrated that "the decisive factor is *not* the speed of transformations but the efficiency of the means applied; not in the vastness of economic reforms, but in the assurance of full power."[113] Full power will be achieved by substituting for the old armed forces "soldiers of a new formation"[114] and by the emergence of a vanguard party. Relying on military and economic power, the Soviets have consistently recommended to the Nicaraguans, as they have to the Angolans and Ethiopians, that there need be

> no explusion of foreign capital, not only because this would hurt the economic development of Nicaragua, but also because the new character of political power has changed the role of foreign capital and now dictates the conditions for its use.[115]

Finally, the Nicaraguan revolution has shown that the current international situation largely predetermines victory for other revolutionary movements in Central America.[116]

Dual Tactics

Yet the Soviet endorsement of armed struggle in Latin America is not absolute: "In some countries and under certain conditions the possibility of winning power by non-violent means has not been invalidated by the fascist coup in Chile."[117] Thus the Soviets are pursuing dual tactics throughout Latin America. In certain countries, like Argentina, Brazil, and Mexico, where the prospects for armed struggle are poor and where those for profitable economic relations are bright, the Soviets seek to broaden commercial and governmental ties and pursue reformist, united front tactics. If the aim is revolution, the main objective is the "unity of left-wing forces." But if reforms or self-perservation are the goals, priority is placed on "unity with the liberal bourgeoisie, with reformists . . . with ruling circles or with traditional parties."[118] Nonetheless, "in most Latin American countries and the region as a whole, the unity of the left-wing forces is the main and decisive factor. . . ."[119]

Nor has the military coup been abandoned as an element in Soviet strategy; it has only been dressed in a new uniform. Whereas previously the military coup was assimilated into the policy of peaceful transition, now it has become a form of armed struggle:

> In a series of countries where patriotic military governments ascended to power . . ., there was no spilling of blood. But in any case there was an application of military force, a fact which converts this course too in an armed road.[120]

Thus, according to another Soviet authority, there are two realistic ways of seizing power:

> that of armed struggle and destruction of the old political and military system, or . . . through a *coup d'etat* . . . with subsequent control over the army.[121]

Although the Soviet tactical line for Latin America has been transformed, the Soviets still preserve the advantages of the low risk policy of the earlier period. With Cuba in tow and with insurgency mounting in Central America, the Soviets can remain in the background and avoid direct confrontation with the United States. The Soviets move cautiously in Latin America, out of cunning, not restraint. While Soviet probes in the region do not signify an independent threat to U.S. security, they are more serious precisely because they are components of and subordinate to Soviet global strategy.

Soviet Strategic Objectives

Soviet strategic objectives in Latin America are multiple. In the Caribbean Basin they seek to establish a naval presence effective enough to threaten any NATO contingency plans to relieve Western Europe from U.S. gulf ports. Such an offensive interdiction capability would bolster the Soviet effort to demonstrate to West European countries that the United States is both unwilling and unable to offer them effective assistance in a crisis.

The severing of the Atlantic alliance is the cardinal objective of the present Soviet strategic deployment. In the mid-1970s the Soviets initiated a long flanking movement directed at the maritime life lines of Western Europe. They have now secured naval facilities adjacent to the Red Sea, the Persian Gulf, and the African sea-lanes. To establish a naval stranglehold on Western Europe, the Soviets must be able to present a threat to maritime traffic in the South Atlantic. This is a major reason for persistent Soviet interest in Argentina, where the Soviets have sought facilities in both Ushuaia off the Beagle Channel and in Puerto Madryn on the Atlantic Coast. During their 1975 worldwide naval exercises (OKEAN), Soviet warships using facilities in Cuba and the Azores demonstrated that they could obstruct the South Atlantic. Cuban-based Soviet ships participated simultaneously in exercises designed to interdict the North Atlantic shipping lanes essential for U.S.-European trade.

The Soviets apparently wish to pursue a strategy of

strategic denial in the Western Hemisphere similar to their Indian Ocean Basin strategy. The Caribbean, the Panama Canal, the Atlantic Narrows, and the sea-lanes around the southern tip of South America are potential choke points where Soviet navy and submarine forces could disrupt the flow of raw materials to the United States. The Soviet bloc naval deployment in the Caribbean, the west coast of Africa, and in the Scotia sea in Antarctica as well as Soviet efforts to gain leverage in Central America may portend a threat to these vulnerable routes. The Soviet support of the internationalization of the Panama Canal rather than Panamanian sovereignty suggests a desire to exercise influence over this key waterway. The Panamanian representatives to the United Nations have censured the Soviet position.

In the shorter term the Soviet aim in the region seems to be to tie down the United States in its own backyard by fomenting interregional conflict. To the extent that the United States is diverted by problems in its strategic rear, the Soviets will have a freer hand in areas of more immediate strategic interest, above all the Indian Ocean Basin.

For these purposes, the opportunities are plentiful for the Soviet Union—not only in Central America but also in the numerous simmering territorial conflicts throughout Latin America. The Soviets, past masters at exploiting troubled borders in Africa and Asia for their own ends, already have issued policy statements favoring one side or another in many of Latin America's interstate conflicts. The general instability of the region, notably in Central America and the Caribbean, is for the Soviets "troubled waters" into which they now have cast their lines.

5

The Sovietization of Cuba

The subjection of the Cuban revolution has been the Soviets' supreme accomplishment in Latin America. Cuba has already proved a crucial asset for Soviet expansion in Africa, and it is the sine qua non of current Soviet Latin American strategy. The Soviet Union has in turn become as indispensable to the Cuban economy as Cuba is to the Soviet's Third World deployment. The current relationship, which some call a partnership (but is much more like clientage than partnership), was not coterminous with the Cuban revolution. On the contrary it took more than a decade and a half before Cuba could be said to be Sovietized and Fidel Castro, in Maurice Halperin's apt phrase, "tamed."[122]

Cuba Independent

In the 1960s, in the first decade after the Cuban revolution, Cuba enjoyed considerable autonomy. Castro was free to pursue an economic policy that disregarded the Soviet canons with respect to the primacy of material incentives, the regulating role of the law of value, centralized planning bodies, and the socialist international division of labor. The Soviets chafed but could do little when Castro, with the arbitrariness of a Latin American *caudillo,* extravagently wasted Soviet assistance on his pet projects. Nor could they deflect his attacks on old-line Cuban Communist Party leaders, on the "servile men" of the local Latin American Communist parties, or on the Soviet Union itself with which Castro differed sharply on most doctrinal and political questions. This autonomy was eventually dissipated as Castro's squandering of political and economic resources finally forced him, in the face of unremitting U.S. hostility, to capitulate to the other superpower, which patiently waited in the wings.

The forging of firm ties of dependency was a complex and protracted process. After an initial period of Soviet reticence, by 1961 planning offices modeled on Soviet ones had been established. Old-line Communist party officials held leading positions along with Fidelistas in an amalgamated, rough imitation of a Communist party, and Castro declared himself a "Marxist-Leninist." Soviet magazines and pamphlets were prominently displayed in newsstands, Soviet manuals were employed in high school and university courses, and Soviet-Cuban trade soared. But after the unilateral Soviet withdrawal of their missiles in October 1962, Soviet-Cuban relations cooled considerably, and the Soviets had to accustom themselves to harsh attacks on peaceful coexistence and peaceful transition, on traditional Latin American Communist parties, on the USSR in its dispute with China, and to the purging of Communists from the Cuban party and state apparati.

Between 1963 and 1965 an unsteady détente existed. Castro visited the Soviet Union twice, fulsomely praising the Soviet leaders. Even though Castro inclined to the Soviet side in the Sino-Soviet dispute, he refused to identify himself completely with Soviet positions and refrained from publicly criticizing Albania and China. He remained critical of the Soviet pursuit of friendly relations with the United States and refused to sign the partial nuclear test ban treaty. At a 1964 meeting of Latin American Communist parties in Havana, which implicitly recognized Cuban leadership in the region, a temporary compromise was reached: The parties agreed to back armed struggle in six countries, including Venezuela, but generally approved peaceful transition elsewhere in Latin America.

In this period Che Guevara, in a widely publicized speech at the February 1965 meeting of Afro-Asian Solidarity in Algiers, accused the Soviet Union of "complicity with the exploiting countries of the West."[123] Guevara, however, who had become something of a supporter of Chinese positions, disappeared from public view shortly thereafter, and the decline of his influence removed a major obstacle in Cuban-Soviet relations. Guevara's program of rapid industrialization was dropped, and Castro adopted economic programs that accorded with Soviet policies, particularly those reestablishing sugar exports as the cornerstone of the Cuban economy and stressing material rather than moral incentives.

The short-lived Soviet-Cuban harmony was ruptured by the U.S. invasion of Santo Domingo in April 1965. Arguing that the invasion was the beginning of an American backlash, the Soviets redoubled their advocacy of the defensive tactics of peaceful transition and united fronts.[124] The uneasy compromise of 1964 had broken down when Soviet-Cuban polemics over armed struggle resurfaced at the Tricontinental Conference of Third World liberation forces in Havana in January 1966.

There the breach was extended beyond Latin America when Castro backed Che Guevara's slogan of creating "two, three, many Vietnams." Castro had already begun to criticize the Soviets for refusing to take "the necessary risks for

Vietnam,"[125] clearly wary that Soviet reticence in that struggle, like the backdown in 1962, boded ill should the U.S. backlash strike Cuba. The Tricontinental Conference inaugurated a period in which Cuba looked for international support to Vietnam, North Korea, Third World national liberation groups, and Latin American guerrilla movements rather than to the Soviet Union and traditional Communist parties. Castro went out of his way to disparage the Chilean Popular Unity front as useful only as a negative example, and branded the old-guard Cuban Communists as "servile men" only adept at copying the experience of others.

Having refused to participate in the Soviet-organized preparatory conference of Communist parties in Budapest in 1967, Castro's break with pro-Soviet Latin American parties was virtually institutionalized at the meeting of the Organization of Latin American Solidarity (OLAS) in Havana in August 1967. There Castro attacked those "antiquated" parties for betrayal of the revolution and conspiring against Cuba. He accused Soviet bloc countries of "aiding the oligarchs" of Latin America by pursuing economic ties.[126]

The Soviets reacted by sharply reducing their 1967 military assistance to Cuba and by slowing down their oil deliveries at a time of record petroleum production in the Soviet Union. Castro retaliated with speeches on the necessity of self-reliant economic development and by blaming gas rationing on the Soviet Union. The "microfaction" of Soviet supporters in the Cuban party was arrested and charged not only with libeling the party as adventurist and petty-bourgeois—echoing similar Latin American Communist party and Soviet criticisms—but also with having maintained illicit relations with the Soviet Union. The faction was charged with encouraging the Soviet Union to impose economic sanctions on Cuba. This was a thinly veiled accusation of Soviet interference in Cuba's internal affairs. As the crisis reached a climax in the spring of 1968, the Cuban press published favorable reports of what came to be known as the "Prague spring."

Cuba Yields

Without access to Cuban and Soviet state papers, there can be no precise account of Castro's sudden about-face after the Soviet occupation of Czechoslovakia. It may be that Castro saw in the Brezhnev Doctrine a promise of protection for his troubled regime. Perhaps mounting difficulties in the Cuban economy and the defeat of one Latin American guerrilla movement after another led Castro to decide that, by extending his support at a time of universal repudiation of Soviet action, he could win more favorable terms in what he now saw as an unavoidable accommodation with his Soviet patrons. In all events, it is now clear that the historic year of 1968 was for Cuba, too, a watershed. That year marked the end of Cuban opposition to the Soviets on major international questions and the beginning of a process in which Cuba would gradually yield one sphere after another of its domestic and foreign policy to Soviet tutelage, a year in which the Cuban revolution's original, fundamental goal of autonomous political and economic development would be abandoned.

Cuba's accomodation to the Soviet Union—a far more accurate term than rapprochement—proceeded in slow but steady stages. Castro's endorsement of the Czechoslovakian occupation was still accompanied by certain criticisms of the Soviets for permitting a "degeneration" not only in Czechoslovakia but in the Soviet Union itself. Although Cuba participated in the International Conference of Communist and Workers' Parties in Moscow in June 1969, its delegation reiterated some of its criticisms of the Latin American parties and did not sign the joint declaration.[127] Nonetheless the Soviets did not spurn the rose for the thorns. Relations warmed; visits and contacts multiplied; trade negotiations prospered; and the customary barbs at the Soviet Union and the Latin American Communist parties gradually disappeared from Castro's speeches. *Pravda* began again to excerpt from them extensively. Yet it was not until the early 1970s that the Bear's hug was completed.

In early 1970 Castro obsequiously told a Soviet correspondent that the improvement of Cuban agriculture would "promote the Soviet Union's confidence in our economic plans."[128] Quite the reverse was the result of the colossal and colossally wasteful effort to achieve a 10-million-ton sugar harvest in that year—a goal that Castro had declared a matter of revolutionary honor. In the wake of the disappointing 8.5 million-ton harvest, the Cuban economy was in shambles, its revolutionary honor depreciated, and Soviet patience exhausted. A new wave of Soviet technicians and advisers flooded Cuban planning and administrative offices, and Cuban officials trusted by the Soviets, like Carlos Rafael Rodriguez (a former member of the old pro-Soviet party) and Vice President Osvaldo Dorticos, were given major responsibility for the economy.

Cuban-Soviet Ties Institutionalized

These Cubans and their Soviet councillors proceeded to replace the old ad hoc Cuban-Soviet economic relationship with formal, institutionalized ties. In December of 1970 Rodriguez took a delegation to Moscow for a meeting with officials of the Soviet Central Planning Board, which established the Cuban-Soviet Commission of Economic and Technical Collaboration.[129] The commission was to set economic policy, guaranteeing that no major project would be undertaken in Cuba without Soviet consent. At its founding, Rodriguez commented that the commission would not only coordinate long-range planning and make better use of resources but prepare a "magnificent plan of industrialization" for Cuba, which would be realized in the second half of the decade.[130]

In 1972 Cuba joined the CMEA, and at the end of that year Cuba and the Soviet Union signed a series of agreements rescheduling the Cuban debt, extending further credit to Cuba, and raising the price of Cuban sugar and nickel in bilateral trade. They also included provisions for technical aid to Cuban industry, especially sugar and nickel. The arrangements gave the CMEA countries first call on Cuban sugar and nickel production, providing Cuba with an assured market but also precluding it from taking advantage of market fluctuations and gaining a degree of economic independence from the Soviet bloc. The arrangement also allowed the Soviet Union to devote sugar beet crop land to more remunerative crops and to utilize fully its sugar refineries.[131] In 1976, as a further step in the institutionalization of the "socialist international division of labor," Cuba agreed to link its five-year plans with those of the Soviet Union. Through these measures a full-fledged dependent economic relationship was installed typical of the old international order in which the northern country provides capital and technology for the exploitation of the natural resources of the southern country.

The Soviet-Cuban relationship extended well beyond mere economic dependency. In 1972 and 1973 more than a dozen delegations of party officials from Soviet bloc countries visited Cuba to advise and to monitor the organization of a Soviet-style Communist party. Delegations of Cuban party leaders traveled to Moscow to receive training.[132] In December 1975 the Cuban Communist Party celebrated its first congress, approving a draft constitution modeled on the Soviet Constitution of 1936.[133] The Cuban state apparatus was similarly renovated along Soviet lines. The Cuban intelligence service (the DGI) was purged of all suspected anti-Soviet officers and came under the direct supervision of General Vassiliy Petrovich of the KGB.[134] Cuban trade unions, women's organizations, and election procedures were also remodeled under Soviet guidance, and systematic courses on Marxism-Leninism were installed at all levels of the Cuban educational system and in the military—again under Soviet guidance.[135]

In the course of their ministrations Moscow forged a pro-Soviet lobby among Soviet-trained technicians and military officers and sympathetic state and party officials. They kept company with the watchful Russian "technicians" installed beside each Cuban minister and vice minister,[136] numerous KGB operatives inside and outside the DGI, and several thousand Soviet troops. Together with the bonds of economic dependency these measures constituted an elaborate neocolonial relationship designed to assure Soviet predominance immune to changes in the present leadership. Indeed the Sovietization of the institutions of the Cuban revolution in these years sharply restricted the sphere of Castro's arbitrary, personal, *caudillo* style of leadership.

Soviet efforts bore immediate political fruit. In November 1971 Castro signed a joint communiqué with Soviet Premier Alexsei Kosygin fully endorsing Soviet foreign policy.[137] At the same time Castro accepted the blame for previous conflicts with the Soviet Union, and President Dorticos recognized the USSR as the leading socialist country.[138] In May 1972 Castro opened in his new role as traveling Third World apologist for the Soviet Union with a two-month trip to Africa and Eastern Europe (longer than all of his previous overseas trips together). Formerly in Eastern Europe Castro had

. . . sorted friend from foe by the country's prevailing antagonism toward the USSR; hence, Rumania had been very high in his esteem several years ago. Now the length of stay in each of the Eastern European countries was positively correlated to their orthodoxy and good standing with Moscow.[139]

Throughout the trip he attacked the United States and lavishly praised Cuba's new patrons. In his trip and upon his return Castro expressed his "eternal gratitude" to the Soviet Union and portrayed Cuban-Soviet economic relations as "the most generous and revolutionary possible."[140] He strove to portray Soviet-Cuban relations not as a new and higher form of neocolonial dependency but as fraternal and selfless cooperation between socialist states.

A high point in Castro's sales campaign came at the Fourth Conference of the Heads of State of Non-Aligned Countries in Algiers in September 1973. At the site where Che Guevara eight years earlier had denounced Soviet exploitation of the Third World, Castro delivered a panegyric on the Soviets' "glorious, heroic and extraordinary services rendered the human race" and championed the Soviet view of a world composed of two antagonistic camps: the imperialist, led by the United States, and the socialist, led by the Soviet Union. [141] He assailed the opposing view that the Soviet Union, like the United States, was imperialistic.[142]

Castro's defense of "two camps" vs. "two imperalisms" enraged a number of nonaligned delegations including Bolivia, Brazil, and Prince Sihanouk's Cambodia. Sihanouk noted that his regime had been deposed by the U.S.-backed despot Lon Nol, who was immediately recognized by the Soviet Union. Castro's most vigorous opponent was Libya's Colonel Mu'ammar Qadhafi, who contended that Cuba had now become a part of the Soviet Union like Uzbekistan and Czechoslovakia and challenged its right to remain in the nonaligned movement:

In the beginning the aim of the revolution was to obtain Cuba's freedom. This freedom has no meaning if it consists of moving from the domination of one power to that of another power. . . . Castro is aligned.[143]

The quarrel with Qadhafi was patched up at the close of the conference by Castro's promise to sever relations with Israel. As Maurice Halperin has written,

> In exchange for breaking relations with Israel, Castro purchased Arab tolerance for the Soviet position and his defense of it, safeguarded his new role as the foremost "nonaligned" champion of the Kremlin, and improved his own leadership aspirations in an increasingly important sector of the Third World. . . . Later, when Russo-Egyptian relations deteriorated, the USSR would find Castro a valuable asset in promoting a new pro-Soviet alignment with Libya and other "progressive" Arab states.[144]

Cuban-Soviet Military Ties

Castro was proving an inestimable political asset for the Soviet Union, but the Soviet investment in Cuba had more extensive aims. On January 1, 1969, the Soviets announced that they had reequipped the Cuban armed forces.[145] A new stage had been inaugurated in Soviet-Cuban military relations in which Soviet assistance passed beyond guaranteeing Cuba's territorial integrity to the construction of a new and formidable component of the emerging Soviet global offensive.

July 1969 saw the first visit of a Soviet naval squadron to Cuba, a visit described by *Red Star* as a "graphic illustration of the combat unity between the Soviet and Cuban Armed Forces."[146] By the end of 1972, Soviet warships had visited Cuba ten times.[147] On their ninth visit the Soviets

quietly slipped a Golf-II conventionally powered, nuclear
ballistic missile-equipped submarine and tender into the
Cuban port of Nipe for servicing.[148] The Soviets were in the
process of establishing by slow, steady stages a significant
naval presence in the Caribbean—indirectly by building up
the Cuban navy and directly by ever longer and larger Soviet ship visits. The process has been described as a classic
example of Soviet incrementalism—an approach that includes

> the elements of a gradual, purposeful buildup ... as well
> as the strategic use of favorable opportunities when
> presented . . . Inherently low-risk in nature, this strat-
> egy seeks steady success in the long run at the expense
> of larger triumphs. . . . [T]he plan calls for the setting of
> an initial precedent which is followed by desensitizing
> regional powers to that action's significance. Once ac-
> complished, another precedent is set and the process
> begins over again.[149]

By 1975 there had been more than a dozen separate Soviet naval deployments to the Caribbean and more than 30
Soviet submarines had called at Cuban ports. These were
coupled with Soviet Bear-D reconnaissance flights off the
U.S. East coast, taking off and landing from Cuban airfields. By 1975 the Soviet and Cuban navies were routinely
exercising together.[150] By 1978 there had been 19 Soviet
naval and naval air deployments to Cuba.

The visits gradually became longer, with a greater number of ships involved. The average length of the first 17 deployments was 38 days, while the 2 in 1978 lasted 65 and 82
days.[151] The most recent visit in April 1981, the first visit
since 1978, included two frigates, an oiler, and a cruiser.[152]
None of these vessels are permanently based in Cuba, but
their visits have rendered the Soviet naval presence a regular feature in the Caribbean. Moreover, this presence has

been accompanied by a similarly incremental Soviet build-up of Cuba's own naval and air forces. The Soviets have slowly but systematically transferred considerable naval craft to Cuba. This transfer has included 28 fast patrol boats armed with Styx missiles, 6 fast Turya hydrofoil boats, 18 Komar patrol boats, 12 OSA guided missile patrol boats, 2 conventional Foxtrot submarines, a diesel powered submarine, and, in August of 1981, a 2,300 ton Koni frigate.[153]

In this period the Cuban armed forces grew to 225 thousand, including an army of 200 thousand, an air force and air defense of 15 thousand, and a navy of 10 thousand, making it the second largest military force in Latin America after Brazil, which has 12 times the population of Cuba.[154] More than 2 percent of the Cuban population is now on active military duty or ready reserve, compared to its Latin American neighbors' average of under .4 percent.[155] The island itself can be said to have become a kind of vast floating military base, united by a Soviet-built central strategic highway and railway system capable of transporting troops and equipment to and from "civilian" airports to "fishing stations" on its coasts. With its Soviet-built, high-speed electronic intelligence system, submarines, MIGs, and fast missile-bearing patrol boats, the Soviet-Cuban military installation in the Caribbean now jeopardizes NATO plans to relieve Western Europe from southern U.S. ports and gives the USSR another area in which to apply pressure in their campaign to splinter NATO.

During the 1970s the Soviets restocked and modernized the Cuban military arsenal. Here again Soviet military assistance displayed a new character. Its purpose was not to protect Cuba against a U.S. invasion—forsworn by the United States in 1962 and in any event proscribed by U.S. involvement in Vietnam and rising antiwar sentiment in the United States—but to prepare a rapid deployment force with legitimacy in the Third World with which to pursue Soviet strategic objectives.

Soviet military advisers, technicians, and instructors arrived with new Soviet military equipment. Accompanying the first ministrations of the notorious Soviet combat instruction brigade, the weaponry, the ranks, and even the uniforms of the Cuban army were Sovietized.[156] The beards of the Cuban soldiers also fell victim to Russification, trimmed off to avoid presenting an anarchistic image on the foreign missions for which they were being prepared. As Cuban troops began to fan out toward Africa in the mid-1970s, the Soviets began to deliver more modern equipment including T-62 tanks, BMP infantry combat vehicles, BM-21 multiple rocket launchers, and ZSU-23-4 self-propelled anti-aircraft guns.[157]

The Cuban airforce was similarly modernized beginning in 1972 with the receipt of a squadron of modern MIG-21s, which renovated the Cuban stock of MIGs.[158] The Soviets built airfields to house these planes and provided AN-26 short-range, TU-154 medium-range, and IL-62 long-range jet transport planes, endowing Cuba with a significant airlift capacity—to be deployed with smashing success in Africa.

Cuba in Africa

The Soviet investment in Cuba reaped rich dividends in Africa. Castro's gift of Cuban youth has been indispensable in advancing the Soviet Union's long-standing and incrementally executed plans for repartitioning Africa. On the scales of history, which weigh only deeds not thoughts, it will make little difference that some Cuban soldiers, like the Christian soldiers centuries earlier in Latin America, understand themselves to be performing "historical" and "brotherly" duties. Yet it is obvious that troops from a small Third

World country with a comparatively unspoiled revolutionary image can do much in Africa that Soviet troops cannot. Revolution and national liberation have prestige and glamour in Africa; superpower meddling and imperialism are detested. The initial Soviet entry into Angola was represented as an independent Cuban initiative for the sake of proletarian solidarity. The Soviet Union, testing the waters, remained as much in the background as possible, though it did introduce large quantities of modern equipment previously unknown in the region and flew more than 45 transport missions and numerous additional passenger sorties in support of the Cuban operations.[159] Even many who retain the belief that Cuba is still essentially autonomous in its foreign and domestic policy acknowledge that

> Cuba could not have quickly deployed a heavily equipped force without Soviet arms shipments to Angola, and eventually Soviet transport. The USSR could not have undertaken a direct combat role itself without risking confrontation with the United States, a deterioration of detente, and charges of Soviet imperialism.[160]

The Soviet role in Africa became more conspicuous after the initial success of the Cuban adventure. In November 1975 the Soviets mounted a major sealift and began to deploy a naval task force of several warships and fleet auxiliaries off the Angolan coast. In the next act of solidarity the Soviet role was more pronounced. Four Soviet generals directed Cuban troops throughout the Ethiopian intervention in 1977.[161] Subsequent Cuban activities in Africa and in the Middle East have been coordinated in an integral package involving other Soviet bloc participants, particularly East German military advisers. Once so proud, so boastful, of the Cuban way of socialism and of revolution, the Castro leadership had reduced Cuba to a docile ward of the world's most powerful and aggressive imperialist.

Impact of Soviet Ties

In the same period that most Latin American countries achieved a degree of political and economic independence unprecedented in their history, Cuba, the "first liberated territory of Latin America," marched in the opposite direction. Economic indices of dependence are virtually unchanged since the Cuban revolution.[162] Export earnings from sugar occupy the same predominant place in the Cuban economy they did 25 years ago, and Cuba is even more a monocultural economy. In 1958 sugar constituted 80 percent of the total exports and 22 percent of the gross national product (GNP). In 1978 those figures were 87 percent and 29 percent respectively.[163]

According to Marxist-Leninist theory, the fundamental purpose of social revolution is to "liberate the productive forces," and yet the Cuban economy has grown at less than .5 percent annually since the revolution.[164] Cuba has cost the Soviet Union $20 billion through 1981, and the CMEA expects to double the value of its economic assistance to the island during the present planning period.[165] The Soviet Union supplies 98 percent of Cuba's oil requirements, the equivalent of three-quarters of its total energy consumption. Castro has said that of the 65 million tons of petroleum needed for the 1981-1985 period, the Soviets have assured them that Moscow will supply 61 million tons.[166]

Soviet participation in Cuba's total market rose from 48 percent in 1975 to nearly 70 percent in 1980, according to Cuba's foreign trade minister, Ricardo Carbrizas Ruiz. Trade between the two countries in the current five-year planning period beginning in 1981 will be half again as great as the previous period, according to an agreement signed in Moscow on October 31, 1980.[167] By 1981 trade turnover with Cuba was equal in value to Soviet trade with West Germany, by far the Soviet's largest nonsocialist trading partner, and constitutes nearly 45 percent of its total trade with the LDCs. [168] The Soviet share in Cuban foreign trade is comparable to that of the United States before 1959, but now it is not only highly concentrated but highly subsidized, implying "deeper subordination than ever in Cuba's economic history, a state from which it cannot withdraw without facing economic chaos at least for the short term. . . ." [169]

The primary Cuban export to the expanding Soviet empire is not sugar but soldiers. In the old colonial societies of Latin America, economic, social, and political life revolved around the main export product. In the Cuba of the 1970s, Soviet aid, training, and supplies contributed to a deepening militarization of Cuban society. Military organizations were upgraded, military academies proliferated, extensive military training was given to students and reservists (who now spend a month and a half per year on active duty), and, at the end of the decade, a new territorial militia was created. An aggressive spirit pervaded the island. This was expressed not only in the fierce intolerance for economic, political, intellectual, and sexual dissidence, which helped to create the conditions for the massive exodus to the United States in 1980, but also by mounting threats and, in one graphic case, hostilities against its neighbors. On May 10, 1980 Cuban bellicosity spilled into the Caribbean when Cuban MIG-21s fired upon and sank a defenseless Bahamanian patrol boat in an unprovoked aggression, machine-gunning the four survivors.

As we have seen, both the failure of Cuban-backed guerrilla *focos* in Latin America and Soviet pressure led Cuba to abandon efforts to foment revolution in Latin America in the late 1960s and to support the Soviet policy of peaceful transition. Thus in the early 1970s Cuba successfully pursued normalization of diplomatic relations with Latin American countries at a time when the area was receptive to such overtures. Nonetheless, even while reestablishing diplomatic and commercial relations, the Cubans were careful to retain clandestine ties with their old associates. Cuba continued to provide them with asylum, training, and other forms of support, though on a smaller scale. By the mid-1970s the Americas Department of the Cuban Communist Party was centralizing covert operations with the DGI under KGB guidance. An integrated network—embracing diplomatic missions, the Cuban official press agency (Prensa Latina), Radio Havana, the Cuban broadcasting service, Cubana Airlines, Cuban military missions, and sympathetic local groups—was deployed under the general leadership of the party's Americas department.

Since 1979, military training to Latin American guerrillas has been reinvigorated. Training courses usually last from three to six months and are accompanied by political indoctrination. More than a dozen schools have been established on the Isle of Youth for imparting political instruction to students from Latin America, Africa, and the Middle East.[170] Unlike the period of the 1960s Cuban intervention in Latin America now counts on Soviet support, more sophisticated political tactics, and a complex and coordinated political, military, propaganda, and intelligence infrastructure. This apparatus focused first on the Caribbean.

6

The Soviet-Cuban Offensive in the Caribbean

Central America, Panama, Mexico, the Caribbean islands, and the northern tier of South America differ widely in cultural traditions, political history, ethnic and social composition, and economic development. But all the countries belong to a single geopolitical entity, the Caribbean Basin, which embraces the littoral states as well as the islands of the Caribbean. The Caribbean itself commands the Atlantic-Pacific and north-south trade routes.[171] From a strategic standpoint the region must be studied as a whole.

The Strategic Stakes

The importance of the area to the United States cannot be overestimated. Current NATO contingency plans call for the bulk of relief troops and equipment to transit the Caribbean in a European war. The Soviet Backfire bomber, based in Murmansk with a 4,000-kilometer range, now jeopardizes the mid-Atlantic route—especially because of the emerging Soviet naval capability to operate beyond the Greenland-

Iceland-United Kingdom gap.[172] In World War II more than 50 percent of the U.S. supplies to Europe and Africa were shipped from Mexican Gulf ports. In the early phase of the war, German submarines destroyed considerable tonnage in the straits of Florida, even as Allied antisubmarine forces held a two-to-one advantage. Today Soviet submarines have reversed that ratio. Furthermore, the 13 Caribbean sea-lanes all pass through 4 choke points vulnerable to interdiction from Cuba.

The Panama Canal continues to enhance the military and commercial value of the region. Although it is true that supertankers (now being abandoned for economic reasons) and large carriers have outgrown the Canal, its fuel savings advantage has grown more relevant in the last few years, and Canal traffic and revenues are at record highs. During the Korean War 22 percent of all U.S. troops and materials passed through the Canal, and it remains as essential today as it was during the Cuban missile crisis and for troops movements in the Vietnam War. Only 13 of the U.S. Navy's 475 ships are too large for the Canal. The Canal has permitted the United States to maintain a three ocean naval presence with only a one and a half ocean navy.[173]

The Caribbean trade routes carry a steadily mounting cargo of strategic and other raw materials. As economic power grows more diffuse and resources more scarce, the strategic importance of these trade routes can only increase. The U.S. Department of Commerce has calculated that imported raw materials will rise from 20 percent of total U.S. raw material consumption to nearly 50 percent by the year 2000.[174] The Caribbean serves as a transshipment point for raw materials flowing from the Middle East, southern Asia, and Africa to the United States. Its high-density oil routes carry more than 50 percent of U.S. oil imports. About 25 percent of imported U.S. oil is refined abroad, more than half of it in Caribbean refineries. If we add to its crucial sea routes and refineries the presence of two major oil producers, Mexico and Venezuela, the aggregate significance of the Caribbean for U.S. oil imports can be said to rival that of the Persian Gulf itself.

The combination of a Soviet naval presence in the Caribbean with a burgeoning Soviet-supplied Cuban navy regularly participating in joint exercises has created a major integrated offensive interdiction capability for Soviet-bloc power in the Caribbean.[175] Soviet Navy Fleet Admiral Sergei Gorshkov visited Grenada in 1980, and there were unconfirmed reports about Soviet intentions to build naval facilities there as well.[176] The Nicaraguan government has confirmed reports that a Soviet floating workshop, designed for ship repair, will be operating off Nicaragua's Pacific coast.[177]

When German U-boats in World War II raised havoc in the straits of Florida and Panama—sinking 260 merchant ships in little more than six months, half of which were oil tankers—they were operating 4,000 miles away from their base in the Bay of Biscay without air cover or direction.[178] At that time Cuba with its small navy was an ally of a United States, able to avail itself of what U.S. Admiral Alfred Thayer Mahan called Cuba's "wholly unique condition among islands of the Caribbean" both as a base of naval operations and as a source of supply to a fleet. On Cuba, Mahan wrote,

> supplies can be conveyed from one point to the other, according to the needs of a fleet by interior lines, not exposed to the risk of maritime capture. The extent of the coastline, the numerous harbors, and the many directions from which approach can be made minimize the danger of total blockade to which all islands are subject.[179]

Today, of course, these assets belong to the Soviet Union, affording it not only a base for submarines in case of war but also aircover. It is clear that by incremental steps, the Soviets have moved within reach of a major strategic objective. As Admiral Gorshkov, architect of the Soviet naval offensive, has stated,

> To achieve superiority of forces over the enemy in the main sector and pin him down in the secondary sectors . . . means to achieve sea control in a theater or a sector of a theater . . . the enemy will be paralyzed or constrained in his operations . . . and thereby hampered from interfering with our operations.[180]

Even now in a European war U.S. convoys could be traced by the large Soviet telecommunication facility in Cuba and disrupted by the Soviet-Cuban navy and air force. To counter this threat the United States would have to destroy the military bases on Cuba, and, short of a nuclear attack, this might well require an invasion. Given Cuba's exceptional Soviet-built air defenses and its own considerable military force, as well as the USSR's Caribbean naval presence, this would be no easy task. One military expert has compared it—rather optimistically at that—to the invasion of Okinawa in 1945, which required over 100 thousand troops and 15 aircraft carriers.[181] Under these circumstances it is understandable why Admiral Harry Train, supreme allied commander Atlantic, envisions deploying one of the scarce U.S. carrier task forces in the Caribbean in the event of an Atlantic war.

The Soviet naval presence in the Caribbean advances another Soviet strategic objective. It is integral to a combined economic, diplomatic, political, and military strategy designed to hasten what Admiral Gorshkov calls "progressive changes" in the region.[182] By showing the flag, the Soviets demonstrate

> the achievements of Soviet science, technology and industry. Soviet mariners, from rating to admiral, bring to the peoples of other countries the truth about our

socialist country, our Soviet ideology and culture and our Soviet way of life.[183]

The Political-Ideological Offensive

The Soviet-Cuban combined military presence has been but one element in Cuba's now activist Caribbean policy. Indeed Cuba's most immediate threat to the region is not military but political. In the second half of the 1970s a Soviet-Cuban regional offensive unfolded, aimed at gaining a foothold in one after another of the eastern Caribbean island chain, which arches eastward toward Europe and Africa and southward toward Guyana, Surinam, and Venezuela.

Cuba's political and ideological offensive in the Caribbean has been favored by three indigenous factors: the region's grinding poverty, anti-Yankee sentiment, and the consolidation of a new radicalized middle class. The latter, schooled in English and in U.S. universities, is among the chief trophies of Cuba's political-ideological campaign in the Caribbean. The campaign has turned to account judiciously designed tours of the island, dozens of schools for foreign students on the Isle of Youth and elsewhere, and such quality cultural exports as professional sports teams, stylish modern jazz recordings and concerts, African folk music festivals, the Cuban National Ballet, and elysian revolutionary films. These have been used along with Cuban teachers, doctors, engineers, agronomists, soldiers, and "advisers" to sympathetic local political groupings and factions.

The whole effort is supplemented by a sophisticated Soviet-tutored intelligence network fed by local sympathizers who also add a touch of local color to Cuban propaganda, which is far more effective than the staid Soviet variety. Besides rearing a fifth column of apologists and agents, these methods help to fashion a general public image of Cuba and its Soviet bloc allies as revolutionary pioneers in a joint struggle against U.S. imperialism. Regimes and movements associated with Cuba thereby become authentic participants in a common revolutionary enterprise. No matter if the economy is in shambles, mundane measurements like growth rates are scarcely relevant to revolutionary processes like those of Jamaica in the 1970s and Grenada today. "The Cuban connection," as Anthony Maingot, the Caribbean specialist, has observed, "operates as a sort of smokescreen covering up deficiencies and incompetencies of all kinds. It is a significant element in the ability of the middle class leadership . . . to stay in power."[184]

Cuban efforts in the Caribbean focused on Prime Minister Michael Manley's left-leaning Jamaican regime in the late 1970s. The Cubans sought to bolster the growing left-wing of Manleys' People's National Party (PNP), led by D. K. Duncan and Hugh Small, while supporting the new Marxist-Leninist Workers Party (WPJ). The WPJ influenced the leftist faction of the PNP, which in turn sought to pressure its own leadership. Both the WPJ and the Duncan-Small faction of the PNP were originally schooled by Dr. Trevor Monroe, a political science professor at the University of the West Indies in Jamaica. In the late 1960s students and teachers at the university came in contact with members of the Black Power movement in the United States and with leaders of emerging African nations.[185] Dark-skinned Jamaicans became the object of Cuban propaganda, which stressed the island's "historic ties" with Black Africa. Monroe was an important figure in the effort to identify the university-based movement with Cuba, and later editions of *The Caribbean Political Source Book*, edited by Monroe, took on the coloration of Soviet manuals.[186]

While Castro and other Cuban officials cultivated warm relations with PNP leaders, Jamaican security officers and youth received military training in Cuba.[187] The Cuban mission in Jamaica expanded under the direction of Ambassador Ulises Estrada, former deputy chief of the Cuban Communist Party's Americas Department and a veteran intelligence operative.[188] Moonex International, a Cuban front corporation with a subsidiary in Jamaica, was involved in a plan to ship ammunition into Jamaica from Miami. The local manager of the corporation was apprehended while fleeing the country, along with Estrada and the Jamaican minister of national security.[189] These events contributed to the electoral backlash that defeated the PNP in the fall of 1981.

Thereupon Grenada became the main focus of Cuban attention. In Grenada, as in Jamaica, "the coincidence between Cuban interests and the interests of radicalized middle class groups bent on holding on to state power is clearly evident."[190] Many of the leaders of the New Jewel Movement, which seized power in March 1979, were middle-class intellectuals educated in Great Britain and the United States. The New Jewel Movement carried out its coup immediately after its leader, Maurice Bishop, had returned from a trip to Cuba. Offering short-term redistribution policies—low-cost housing, milk programs for children and pregnant women—and in sharp contrast to its grossly corrupt predecessor, the new government quickly won a following among urban youth. It banned the Grenadian "Back to Africa" Rastafarian movement, suppressed both nongovernment newspapers (the influential *Torchlight* and *The Catholic Forces*), and indefinitely suspended elections. These measures were rationalized with Soviet-style slogans about the irrelevance of bourgeois democracy to the struggle for socialism and the noncapitalist road. In addition, the Cubans have uniformed, armed, and trained a Grenadian army of 2,000, which is kept in military zones declared off-limits to the local population. With a total population of only 110 thousand—Grenada probably has the highest ratio of troops to civilians of any country in the world.[191]

Cuba dispatched Julian Torres Rizo, a senior intelligence officer from the Americas Department, as ambassador to Grenada and supervisor of the numerous Cuban-advised programs on the island. Torres Rizo enjoys close relations with Bishop and other important Grenadian government officials.[192] Cuban programs on Jamaica include military, security, technical, and propaganda assistance. Havana is helping in the construction of a prefabricated cement plant and a 75-kilowatt transmitter for Radio Free Grenada. Several groups of Grenadian students are currently studying in Cuba.[193] Trade relations between the two islands are flourishing, and Cuban and Grenadian officials have been discussing the establishment of a joint Cuban-Grenadian trade commission.[194] Diplomatic, cultural, and economic relations with the Soviet Union have also prospered.[195]

The most tumultuous issue in U.S.-Grenadian relations has been the construction of an airport with a 9,800-foot runway at Port Salines by more than 300 Cuban construction workers using Soviet equipment. The Grenadian government argues that the runway is needed to handle international jetliners in the expansion of its tourist industry, despite Bishop's program to discard "the baggage of decadent bourgeois society." More to the point is the question of whether Cuba would have gone to so much trouble if the venture did not promise military benefits. What is clear is that such an airport could accomodate any aircraft in the Soviet-Cuban arsenal and would extend the combat radius of Cuba's MIG-23s to Venezuela, Guyana, Surinam, and Colombia. It could also provide the Cubans and Soviets with a perfect staging area for operations in the northern tier of South America and solve Cuban problems in obtaining secure refueling stops for military flights to Africa.

It is not hard to imagine circumstances in which this potential could materialize. Bishop's Grenada has signed trade and technical agreements with the Soviet Union and other CMEA nations as well as with West European countries, and actively supports Soviet foreign policy. Grenada was the only Latin American country besides Cuba to oppose the January 1980 U.N. resolution calling for Soviet withdrawal from Afghanistan. Only ten Third World countries—plus states like Mongolia, Vietnam, and Angola—supported the USSR. Even Nicaragua abstained. Such a display of support does not leave much room for confidence in how Grenada may choose to use its new airport. In any event, Grenada is hardly the source of the Caribbean security problem, and making a major issue over the airport will not help the United States in a region where economic problems are so widespread and profound.

The economies of the microstates composing the Leeward and Windward islands have long been dependent on tourism as well as on the now flagging exports of agricultural products. The peoples of these countries are observing the progress of the Grenadian revolution and are awaiting the results of the Reagan administration's "Caribbean Basin Initiative," an economic package proposed by President Ronald Reagan in February 1982, with keen interest. The Grenadian leadership has close relations with the leadership of many left-wing movements in neighboring islands. Should the Caribbean Basin Initiative fail, producing a backlash resulting from awakened, then unfulfilled, expectations, the Grenadian model will become more relevant. With their weak security forces, many of these island governments could be overthrown with minimum military effort transforming the regional balance of power.[196]

Havana and Moscow may well perceive an opportunity for penetration in the territorial dispute between Guyana and Venezuela over Essequibo. Guyana has enjoyed close but erratic relations with the Soviet Union and Cuba for a decade, having been, according to Soviet publicists, "one of the first countries in [the Caribbean] region to establish diplomatic relations and promote cooperation with the Soviet Union, Cuba and other socialist countries."[197] In 1977 Guyana applied for "formal association" status in the CMEA, but the application has not been accepted because of East European reluctance to assume the economic burdens of another underdeveloped country.[198]

At this time Essequibo became the site of Reverend Jim Jones's People's Temple. Reportedly the Guyana government stipulated that the American sect's Jonestown settlement be located 20 miles from the Venezuelan border in Essequibo to establish and tighten the government's control over the disputed zone.[199] The People's Temple had longstanding relations with the Soviet Union and reportedly was negotiating with both Cuba and the Soviet Union about a move to one of those countries just before the Jonestown disaster.[200] Between 1976 and 1978, relations between Guyana and Cuba were especially warm, the former permitting the latter to refuel its Africa-bound transport planes in Guyanese territory. At that time, up to 200 Cuban technicians, advisers, and medical personnel were stationed in Guyana.[201]

The harmony was broken in the summer of 1978 with Guyanese charges of Cuban and Soviet involvement in a major sugar strike. In August 1978, five Cuban diplomats were expelled. Guyana was also reportedly displeased with Cuba for allegedly cheating on an agreement granting fishing rights. In addition, Guyana was said to be disappointed with the meager Soviet economic assistance.[202]

Recently relations have warmed. Aeroflot planes have been refueling in Guyana en route to Nicaragua, and the Soviets have publicly been urging the two major Guyanese political parties, both of which describe themselves as Marxist-Leninist, but which are actually based on racial divisions among Guyana's black and East Indian population, to unify into "a single front of national patriotic forces" in "socialist oriented Guyana."[203] On May 20, 1981, Castro announced official support for the Guyanese position.[204] Two months later Cuba opened up a credit line for Guyanese purchase of industrial equipment, while U.S.-Guyanese relations deteriorated as a result of a U.S. veto of an Inter-American Development Bank loan to Guyana on the grounds that its economy was too "statist."

Venezuelan authorities claim that Havana has sent military advisers to Guyana and allege increased military activity in the Essequibo area. Should hostilities break out and Cuba wish to harass Venezuela, the airfield in Grenada would provide a perfect staging area for amphibious operations. Cuba has provided military training to Guyana's People's Militia and, in the summer of 1981, Guyana acquired two 65-foot Soviet-built fast patrol boats.[205]

Cuba has also cast an eye on the neighboring island of Hispaniola, shared by the Dominican Republic and Haiti. The chief of the Dominican Republic's National Department of Intelligence asserts that his department has detected numerous Cuban operatives in the Dominican Republic, which, he asserts, holds a "marked interest" for Cuba.[206] The U.S. State Department also claims that

> since early 1980, the Cubans have been encouraging radicals in the Dominican Republic to unite and prepare for armed actions. Cuban intelligence officials, like Omar Cordomba Rivas, chief of the Dominican Republic desk of the [Cuban Communist Party's] Americas Department, make periodic visits to the islands.[207]

These recent efforts supplement increased Soviet bloc programs to attract Dominican students, and, in July 1981, the pro-Soviet Dominican Communist Party for the first time publicly announced a Soviet scholarship program for more than 100 students annually.[208]

Cuba has for some time also been hosting Haitian exiles. Naturally, U.S. "complicity" with the repressive Haitian regime makes Haiti a more vulnerable and more attractive target for the Cubans. As in El Salvador, the dilemma for U.S. policy is obvious: How can the United States oppose Soviet-Cuban penetration without also opposing legitimate and inevitable domestic movements to alter an intolerable status quo, and how can the United States oppose Soviet hegemonist designs without seeming to restore American hegemony?

7

The USSR, Cuba, and
the Central American Revolution

Central American revolutionary movements were not created by the Soviet Union and Cuba but are a historical product of Central America's backward, repressive, oligarchical, and dependent societies. As late comers to the Central American crisis, Soviet and Cuban influence was for a long time marginal. As new social forces took up age-old grievances in Central America, all democratic channels were blocked or suppressed. That is what gave the Soviet Union and Cuba their golden opportunity.

Even more than in their early involvement in Africa, the Soviet Union has remained on the sidelines—coaching, cheering, and bankrolling. For one thing, direct involvement would destroy the argument that the USSR seeks only to preserve spheres of influence and is not interested in expansion. Obvious Soviet meddling in America's backyard would legitimize U.S. support for Afghani insurgents and Polish workers. It would violate the rules of the game that the Soviets make a show of observing. Moreover, Soviet intervention could arouse the same Latin American antiimperialist sentiment Moscow seeks to focus against the United

States. The Cuban champions of antiimperialism take the risks that international solidarity requires. Thus Cuba has been actively involved in training, supplying, and helping to unify the insurgent movements. But these seeds would have struck barren soil had Central America itself not been in the midst of a profound upheaval.

Winds of Change

The previous status quo in Central America rested on a relatively immobile socioeconomic structure, authoritarian military governments monopolizing armed power, the allegiance of the Catholic church, an economic dependence on the United States, and, in the last instance, recourse to U.S. intervention. All of these pillars have cracked in the last several years; some have crumbled altogether.

In the past three decades the modernization of the export sector, efforts at import-substitution industrialization, and the Central American common market have energized the region's economies. Annual GNP grew at more than 5 percent, the labor market expanded steadily, per capita income doubled, and exports increased sixteenfold.[209] Both the internal and external market widened, a manufacturing sector developed, and productivity and output grew steadily.[210] The urban population expanded from 16 percent in 1950 to 43 percent in 1980.[211]

Under the social and political conditions prevailing in Central America, however, economic growth was not a force for stability. Some of the appurtenances of the twentieth century appeared on the Central American landscape. While the old landlords and a small rural bourgeoisie prospered, the producers suffered a dramatic deterioration in their living standards. In the 1960s the expansion of the export sector generated pressure on scarce available land, nearly quadrupling rents charged to peasants.[212] Large numbers of peasants were forced to join the growing class of landless laborers. Currently, less than half of the Central American rural population lives on *minifundia* of fewer than 10 acres, and more than a third are landless.[213] Peasants migrated to cities in search of work, but the industrial expansion was limited by the import of relatively capital-intensive technology and by the restricted size of Central American markets. Real wages declined—in Guatemala, for example, they fell by an estimated 25 percent between 1972 and 1977. Natural disasters like the earthquakes in Nicaragua and Guatemala and hurricane Fifi in Honduras took a toll paid mainly by the poor. The latter constitute a disproportionate share of the population in what have become the most inequitable societies in Latin America.[214] The Central American countryside, which several years ago the United Nations compared with the poorest of the poor—countries like Somalia, Bangladesh, and Haiti— with its shantytowns of landless migrants, began to surround cities where the wealthy seek sanctuary in armored cars and behind guarded, electrified walls. As regional economic growth slowed in the late 1970s, a major crisis had already begun.

With the partial exception of Costa Rica, whose distinctiveness is growing precarious, the socioeconomic conditions of the countries of Central America are as proximate as their location. The same is true of their political histories. Pressure for agrarian reform began to build in Nicaragua, Guatemala, El Salvador, and Honduras during the late 1960s. Agrarian reform was one of the demands common to the economic and political reform movements that emerged nearly simultaneously in each of these countries in the early 1970s. They suffered similar fates. In 1972 the Salvadoran electoral coalition led by Napoleon Duarte and Guillermo Ungo was deprived of victory by fraud and by a subsequent military coup. The populist reform movement led by young military officers that came to power in Honduras in the same year had been dispersed by 1975. In Guatemala the reform coalition led by General Efrain Rios Montt was robbed of victory by an electoral fraud in 1974.

These movements did not disappear; they were deeply rooted. Economic change had produced a middle class, an urban working class, landless laborers, and masses of impoverished peasants. The Central American church was deeply permeated by new social forces and ideas. The military establishment generally resisted them. Thus, the centuries-old alliance of church and sword was ruptured. Churchmen often became opposition spokesmen, sometimes joining guerrilla movements themselves.

The Sandinista victory in Nicaragua was bound to have a ripple effect throughout the region with its interwoven histories and shared conditions.

> Today, businessmen, political parties, bishops, journalists, right-wing "death squads," generals and guerrillas joined together across borders, in formal organizations and informal networks. Events in any one country now travel quickly across these numerous channels and affect the mood and political calculations of people throughout the region. Weapons, too, flow easily across long and porous borders.[215]

In the past, revolutionary sparks could be extinguished by U.S. police actions. This is no longer the case, in part because those interventions created profound anti-Yankee and powerful nationalist sentiments in all sectors of the population—even among military officers.[216] The agonizing review of military options conducted by the U.S. Defense and State Departments in the fall of 1981 reflected this change of circumstances.[217] This is one of the factors that has led Moscow to celebrate the deterioration of the U.S.

strategic rear and to give Cuba Soviet blessings to fish in troubled waters.

The Sandinista Revolution

Leaders of the small Sandinista movement went to Cuba in the 1960s for refuge and political and military training. By 1977 the Cubans had developed strong ties with all three Sandinista factions. In 1978, perceiving the domestic and regional isolation of the Somoza regime, the Cubans began to intervene more actively. In the summer of 1978, they mediated differences among the Sandinista factions, and in March 1979 they were instrumental in bringing about their unification. They began to provide contacts with international arms dealers and supplied some weapons themselves discreetly, often through the good offices of neighboring countries like Panama and Costa Rica.[218] Panama, Costa Rica, Venezuela, and Mexico may each have contributed more arms to the Sandinistas, but the Cuban role as intermediary and coordinator through operations headquarters in Costa Rica was essential and a harbinger of future activities elsewhere.[219]

In 1979, as the struggle reached a climax, Cuba assisted in the formation, equipping, and transport of an "internationalist brigade" to Nicaragua. Cuban military specialists, maintaining direct radio contact with Havana, were also dispatched to Nicaragua. These operations were coordinated through the Costa Rican headquarters, whose chief, Julian Lopez Diaz of the Americas Department, became the Cuban ambassador to Nicaragua after the Sandinista victory.[220]

By the spring of 1979 the introduction of ground-to-air missiles, mortar, recoilless rifles, and other heavy infantry weapons new to Latin American guerrilla movements had helped to alter the military balance in Nicaragua. They enabled the Sandinistas, without stable base areas, access to major enemy arsenals, or having defeated the National Guard in full-scale confrontations, to abandon protracted war and to pass, with overwhelming mass support, to popular insurrection. Their quick victory heightened Soviet claims about the role of "the new correlation of global forces." Yet theorists of national liberation struggles, including, previously, the Soviets themselves, have regarded protracted war as a school for preparing the masses to exercise power. Moscow has learned that when revolution contains a high import coefficient, the domestic population will be less qualified to participate actively in the future organization of society and will be more vulnerable to outside influences.

Costa Rica, Panama, and Venezuela have all expressed reservations about the evolution of post-revolutionary Nicaragua. Cubans have filled key military, intelligence, and security advisory positions there, leading Panama to withdraw its military advisers with "friendly warnings" on the extent of Cuban influence.[221] Former Presidents Carazo of Costa Rica and Andres Perez of Venezuela have voiced similar concerns about Cuban influence among the Sandinistas.[222]

El Salvador

These preoccupations have altered Cuban activities in support of the Salvadoran insurgency. With the exception of Nicaragua, Cuba cannot rely on El Salvador's neighbors for logistical support. Instead, the Cubans have played a more direct role and have turned, on the one hand, to clandestine groups in those countries and, on the other, to the Soviet bloc and certain Arab countries.

Utilizing ties with local Communist parties, guerrilla groups, and the Sandinista National Liberation Front (FSLN), and employing when possible arms supply channels established for the Sandinistas, the Department of the Americas of the Cuban Communist Party has supervised and coordinated clandestine support networks in Honduras, Costa Rica, and Nicaragua. At the same time Cuba has assisted in the acquisition and the delivery of material from Eastern Europe, Vietnam, Ethiopia, and Nicaragua via surface and air routes and Cuban boats.[223]

It is obvious that such a complex clandestine operation could not occur without Soviet approval. Soviet complicity was apparent in the June 2, 1980 meeting between Shafik Handal, secretary general of the PCS, and Mikhail Kudachkin, deputy chief of the Central Committee of the Soviet Communist Party. At the meeting Kudachkin suggested that Handal travel to Vietnam to acquire arms and offered to pay for the trip. He also requested that the 30 students sent by the PCS for study in Moscow receive military training for participation in the insurgency. Six weeks later, upon returning from Vietnam, Handal met with Karen Brutents, chief of the Latin American section, and was told that the Soviet leadership was inclined to transport the now promised Vietnamese arms.[224] The Soviets kept their involvement indirect but saw that Handal did not return empty-handed from the East. This is perfectly in keeping with the Soviet strategy of low-intensity, proxy warfare in the United States' strategic rear.

After Handal had returned to El Salvador with promises of arms from Vietnam, Ethiopia, Czechoslovakia, and East Germany, the official Soviet party journal, *Kommunist,* printed a long article by Handal, an honor not usually bestowed on the obscure leader of a tiny party.[225] Moscow, by insuring the success of Handal's trip and boosting his reputation in the international Communist movement, sought to bolster the influence of the PCS within the Salvadoran opposition coalition. Given the small size of the Communist party contribution to the FMLN and the anti-Soviet leanings of several of its members, this preferential treatment from Moscow is necessary.[226]

The three most important guerrilla groups in El Salvador all have anti-Soviet origins. The Popular Liberation Forces (FPL) split from the pro-Soviet PCS in 1970 after a long and bitter struggle against Soviet revisionism and reformism. The old Castroite positions of the 1960s have always been strong among them, and anti-Soviet sentiments have been fortified by an important contingent of Christian Socialists. A second major group, the People's Revolutionary Army (ERP), was influenced by the works of Mao Zedong and Korea's Kim Il-Sung. In 1975, its military commission tried and executed the group's leading intellectual, Roque Dalton, on suspicion of being a "Soviet-Cuban and CIA double-agent." When Dalton's supporters protested that they were attacked physically, they requested the mediation of the FPL and subsequently left the ERP to form the Armed Forces of National Resistance (FARN). This episode increased Cuba's weight in the Salvadoran revolutionary movement.

The Cubans now began to condition expansion of their support on "unity of the left," finally consummated at two meetings in Havana in December 1979 and May 1980. Whatever the Soviet-Cuban role in this, it remains true, as Handal affirms in his *Kommunist* article, that "the situation in the country demanded unification of all revolutionary and democratic forces."[227]

Assured of the unity of the guerrilla groups, the Cubans expanded their logistical role and began to assist in tactical planning. Beginning in the summer of 1980, the Cubans aided the Unified Revolutionary Directorate (DRU) in elaborating battle plans that led to the "final offensive" of January 1981.[228] In February 1981 the guerrilla leadership regrouped in Havana to revise their strategy.[229] In August of 1981, a member of the Soviet Communist Party Politburo met with Central American Communist Party leaders and Cuban officials to discuss regional strategy.[230] Nonetheless, suspicions of the Soviet Union, Cuba, and even Nicaragua grew during 1981 in three of the five guerrilla groups composing the Farabundo Marti National Liberation Front (FMLN). The five groups still harbor mutual distrust, hold different strategic views, and retain separate organizational strategies.

Guatemala

A similar pattern is emerging in Guatemala. The Guatemalan Party of Labor, the local pro-Soviet party, echoing the new Soviet line, now maintains that

> unity of the revolutionary forces is the key factor which ensured the victory . . . of the Cuban revolution. In Nicaragua, the overthrow of Somoza was made possible through concerted action by a majority of the left-wing and progressive organizations. . . . A similar process is underway in El Salvador. The lessons of Cuba, Nicaragua and El Salvador say that there must be no exceptions to unity. An attempt to keep out of any revolutionary organization harms the common cause. In Guatemala as well there are conditions for the cohesion of the left-wing forces, although certain difficulties need to be overcome to attain it.[231]

The statement's hints and veiled criticisms indicate that unity of the left is not easy to achieve. Stubborn nationalist sentiment among the revolutionary groups resists outside dictation. This is nowhere more true than in Guatemala.

In November of 1980 four Guatemalan guerrilla organizations—the Rebel Armed Forces (FAR), the Revolutionary Organization of the Armed People (ORPA), the Guerrilla

Army of the Poor (EGP), and the dissident Guatemalan Labor Party (PGT-D) but not the pro-Soviet Guatemalan Labor Party—signed a fragile unity accord. Manuel Pineiro Losada and Ramiro Jesus Abreu of the Cuban Communist Party were present, and a delegation was sent to Moscow to present the agreement to Castro.[232] Nonetheless the unity remains precarious. Bitter divisions persist, and, while there is evidence of a common military strategy, political unity has still not been reached.

The progress toward unity led the Cubans to expand their military assistance and training programs. In a press conference in Guatemala in June of 1981 two captured ORPA guerrillas declared that they had been part of a group of at least 22 Guatemalans who participated in a seven-month military training course in Cuba. The prisoners said they had left via Costa Rica and Panama and returned via Nicaragua and Honduras.[233] Reportedly, arms shipments coordinated by the Cubans are reaching the Guatemalan guerrillas from Nicaragua by way of Honduras.[234] Yet in Guatemala, as in Nicaragua and El Salvador, arms are easily procured from a number of sources, including Miami. The U.S. State Department, however, has stated that M-16 rifles captured from the Guatemalan guerrillas have been traced to those left by U.S. forces in Vietnam, which strongly suggests a Cuban role.[235] Apparently, the guerrillas now have at their disposal submachine guns, rocket launchers, and 50mm. mortars also. Some of these weapons may have been provided by the Salvadoran guerrillas.[236]

Although weapons transfers make headlines, the fundamental issue is not arms but political control. Insurgent groups have traditionally taken arms from wherever they can get them; this does not necessarily mean that the donor will dominate the recipient. It would be foolish to overlook the Soviet-Cuban involvement in equipping Central American guerrilla movements, especially since arms supplies have come to occupy such a central place in Soviet strategy, but we should not draw hasty conclusions. Although some national liberation movements have tasted the bitter fruit beneath the Soviets' sugar-coated generosity, there is an inherent contradiction between national liberation and Soviet hegemonism. Frequently this contradiction does not become apparent until it is too late.

A Soviet Orientation for Nicaragua?

As we saw in chapter 4, Soviet authorities have recently designated Central America as a region in which states of socialist orientation are emerging. The pro-Soviet Nicaraguan Socialist Party has been recommending that Nicaragua pursue a course that closely resembles Soviet prescriptions for socialist orientation.[237] The present Sandinista leadership appears to be receptive, and the mounting Soviet and Cuban influence pulls in the same direction.

The USSR now coordinates the economic, political, operational, and intelligence aspects of military assistance in one tightly managed bureau. The State Committee for Economic and Foreign Relations reports to the military council of the Politburo, bypassing the normal bureaucratic lines and directly linking political and economic objectives to arms sales programs and to the KGB.[238] Elements of this integrated approach can be discerned in Nicaragua.

In March 1980 the FSLN signed a mutual support agreement with the Soviet Communist Party. Such agreements have normally been reserved for parties in regimes that Moscow regards as having a socialist orientation. The agreement, coupled with the revised Soviet judgment that "military-political fronts of the July 26 Movement and the Sandinista Front of National Liberation . . . have shown . . . that they are capable . . . of substituting for the political parties of the proletariat,"[239] suggested Soviet hopes that the FSLN would, under Soviet guidance, become a Soviet-style vanguard party.

The Soviet effort in Nicaragua is beginning to show the characteristics of a now familiar division of labor employed in places like Ethiopia, Angola, South Yemen, Kampuchea, Afghanistan, and Mozambique. As in Angola and Ethiopia, Cuba is acting as the Soviet stalking-horse in Nicaragua. Cuban influence among the Sandinistas reaches back to the first years of the FSLN, for whom the Cuban revolution was a source of inspiration and emulation. Deep-rooted sympathy for the Cuban revolution among both the Nicaraguan people and the Sandinista leadership is one legacy of United States harassment of the Cuban revolution and U.S. support for the Nicaraguan dictator Anastasio Somoza.

Cubans provide combat training for the growing Nicaraguan army, already the largest in Central America.[240] Cuba played a leading role in the literacy campaign as well, by inviting more than 600 Nicaraguan students to its highly politicized educational facilities on the Isle of Youth. Cuban ideological influence is pervasive. *Barricada*, the official Sandinista organ, is modeled on *Granma*, the official Cuban newspaper, and relies on *Prensa Latina*, the Cuban press agency. Like *Nuevo Diario*, the "independent" progovernment paper, it routinely takes Cuban (and Soviet) positions on virtually all international issues from European theater nuclear modernization to Poland, Afghanistan, Libya, and China. Sandinista Defense Committees, imitations of the Cuban Revolutionary Defense Committees, have tended to become FSLN party organs—a network of bosses and ward heelers "exercising vigilance" over comings and goings at the grass roots level. They are now being supplemented by a militia assisted by Cuban advisers.

Direct links with the Soviet Union have proliferated as well. In the fall of 1979 two studies prepared under government direction contemplated replacing Nicaragua's dependency on the U.S. market with ties with the CMEA.[241] These have been revised, apparently in line with Soviet advice to preserve economic relations with the West. The Soviets advocate such relations in Angola and Ethiopia as well—preferring to let the West sustain the economic burden of these underdeveloped countries while they consolidate military and political ties.[242] In late March 1980, the Nicaraguan and Soviet governments signed a series of agreements for economic, technical, scientific, and cultural cooperation, cooperation in the area of planning, and air transport links.[243]

On January 1, 1981 Radio Moscow announced a new scientific and cultural program based on the agreement signed in Moscow in March 1980. It explained that

> implementation . . . began . . . immediately after the victory of the people's revolution in Nicaragua when groups of Soviet specialists in fields of importance to the Nicaraguan economy, such as hydropower engineering, agriculture, geology, nonferrous metallurgy, forestry, fisheries and education came to the country. The recommendations drawn up by Soviet specialists will be taken into account in the drawing up of plans for the economic and social development of the Republic of Nicaragua. . . . In turn, delegations of Nicaraguan specialists in the most varied spheres . . . have visited the Soviet Union. A large group of Nicaraguans are studying in our country. These are the future cadres who are not (immediately) necessary for the restoration of the country.[244]

During 1981 considerable numbers of Nicaraguans were sent to the Soviet Union for training in such areas as telecommunications engineering, medicine, construction engineering, and agriculture.[245] The Soviets and East Europeans also donated wheat and extended credits and soft loans for construction and agricultural machinery, for amplification of radio stations, and for scientific investigation.[246] Nonetheless, Western Europe, Mexico, private Western banks, and several Arab countries have extended far more economic assistance to Nicaragua than has the Soviet bloc.[247]

Of much greater importance has been a series of Soviet-Nicaraguan military agreements. The Soviets have loaned the Nicaraguans two HI8 helicopters and twelve pilot technicians.[248] Soviet T-55 tanks, tank warfare courses from Soviet texts, and Soviet AK-47 rifles are standard.[249] Furthermore, there is evidence that the Nicaraguans have undertaken preparations for the arrival of Soviet MIGs. Other agreements allow the Soviets to operate their floating workshop for ship repair off Nicaragua's Pacific coast.[250] Another provides the Soviets fishing privileges off Nicaraguan waters.

In other countries concessions like these have permitted the Soviets to conduct naval surveillance and have led eventually to naval facilities and bases. Unconfirmed intelligence reports of the transfer of Soviet tankers from Cuba to Nicaragua suggest that the Soviets are taking their customary incremental steps in Nicaragua, coordinating economic, political, and security elements in an integrated strategy of penetration. As in such previous efforts, East Germany, Bulgaria, Vietnam, and other Soviet bloc states are participating in the Nicaraguan buildup.

Nicaragua has not yet joined the Soviet bloc, however. There is resistance to such a step both within the Sandinista front and in the population at large. Nonetheless, Nicaragua's Soviet-assisted military buildup and the concentration of political and ideological power in the hands of pro-Cuban Sandinistas lend credence to the Reagan administration's inflated charges that the country has become another Soviet proxy.

Some observers reject this possibility out of hand, citing Moscow's unwillingness, especially with its current economic difficulties, to assume the burden of another Cuba. They also point to Fidel Castro's advice to the Nicaraguans to preserve both economic links with the West and the domestic private sector. But such complacency ignores the shift in Soviet tactics discussed in chapter 4. As we have seen, Soviet writers have stated that, as a result of the changed correlation of global forces, new conditions prevail in which economic assistance from the Soviet bloc no longer is "a factor directly promoting the transition to a non-capitalist path." Instead, emphasis is placed on "the political, military-strategic and moral influence of the states of the socialist community."[251] In Nicaragua this involves, in addition to Soviet bloc military assistance, a predominant Cuban presence in the military, security, and intelligence apparati of the Nicaraguan government and the collaboration of leading Sandinistas like Defense Minister Humberto Ortega.[252] For Comandante Ortega, the world is divided "into two great camps: one side the camp of imperialism, the camp of capitalism, led by the United States . . . and on the other the socialist camp . . . with the Soviet Union in the vanguard."[253]

As former Nicaraguan Ambassador to the United States Arturo Cruz has put it, the Sandinistas have yet "to make the transition from being soldiers to being political leaders."[254] Many Latin Americans and U.S. Latin Americanists attribute this delay to the youthful pride of successful revolutionaries, coupled with an understandable fear of U.S. intentions. Such a view is sensitive to the causes of Third World revolutions and the deep-rooted misery and oppression that spawns them but is less sensitive to the dire consequences for the countries involved when those revolutions become instruments of Soviet hegemonism. Cognizant of repeated U.S. interference in the Third World, those who hold such views tend to overlook both the systematic, strategic nature of recent Soviet activities and the pervasive Cuban influence among Central American revolutionaries.

The Sandinistas' Soviet-Cuban orientation became increasingly evident in 1981, and by early 1982 many respected Latin American nationalists had spoken out against it. The late General Omar Torrijos of Panama and ex-President Carlos Andres Perez of Venezuela, the Sandinistas two most influential Latin American supporters, voiced strong criticisms, as have most of the democratic parties in the region and leading Latin American members of both the Socialist International and the Christian Democratic World Federation. In February 1982 a meeting of the Socialist International in Caracas was postponed because of Latin American protests against the presence of Sandinista observers. In April, Eden Pastora, the legendary "Comandante Zero," the most popular Sandinista hero, denounced the regime for betraying its commitment to self-determination and nonalignment.

Many of Pastora's former comrades-in-arms and a large number of government officials have resigned their posts, and the Misquito Indians, once opponents of Somoza, have risen in rebellion. A broad national democratic opposition now embraces the only independent newspaper, *La Prensa*, the majority of the clergy, and most political parties that supported the revolution. By harassing the revolution from the outside and seeming to align itself with ex-Somozistas, the United States has undercut this patriotic opposition and revived the failing popular support of the Sandinista government. It remains to be seen whether the United States will join with or eventually subvert the antihegemonist sentiments of the Nicaraguan people and Nicaragua's neighbors.

8

The Cuban Offensive
and Latin American Reaction

The new Cuban offensive has been confined neither to any putative sphere of influence in the Caribbean nor to solidarity with the Central American revolutions. Recent Cuban activity includes assistance to guerrilla groups in Colombia and Chile and hostility toward Venezuela.

Colombia

Colombia renewed diplomatic relations with Cuba in 1975, as did many other countries during the period when Cuba, following Moscow's lead, was pursuing peaceful coexistence with Latin American governments. Nonetheless, Havana, like Moscow, continued to train Colombian guerrilla leaders like Jaime Bateman, founder of the M-19 guerrilla organization. The Cubans also gave instruction to leaders of other Colombian guerrilla groups such as the National Liberation Army (ELN) and the pro-Soviet FARC (Revolutionary Armed Forces of Colombia).[255]

Like many other democratic Latin American countries in

the late 1970s, Colombia maintained full diplomatic and commercial relations with Cuba and supported the Sandinistas against Somoza, permitting Colombian volunteers to join the fight. Nonetheless Castro appears to have soured on Colombia when it chose to run against Cuba for the Latin American seat on the United Nations Security Council in the winter of 1979. Cuba had orchestrated its campaign carefully, especially at the Havana meeting of the non-aligned movement that fall. Castro rancorously labeled Colombia's candidacy "traitorous" and a "shameless maneuver," blaming Colombia, not the Soviet invasion of Afghanistan, for Cuba's failure to win the seat.[256]

In the spring of 1980 when the M-19 held a group of diplomats hostage in the Dominican embassy in Bogota, Havana agreed, as part of a negotiated settlement, to grant the guerrillas asylum in Cuba where the remaining hostages were later released. In official Colombian circles this was welcomed as a generous diplomatic gesture. The actual intention now appears far from generous. The Cubans proceeded to provide the exiled guerrillas with extensive training for what turned out to be the first phase of a Cuban-assisted operation against the Colombian government.

In July of 1980 Cuban intelligence officers arranged a unity meeting of representatives of the rival Colombian M-19, ELN, and FARC guerrilla groups in Panama. Unsuccessful in establishing common strategy and tactics, the meeting did initiate collaboration among the organizations, which has continued to the present. At the end of 1980, with Cuban assistance, the M-19 sent Cuban-trained cadre to Panama to begin preparations for a major operation in Colombia. More than 100 armed guerrillas landed by boat in Colombia in February 1981, where they attempted unsuccessfully to create a people's army. Under questioning, several captured guerrillas admitted to training in Cuba and named five Cuban advisers who had instructed them.[257] When accused by Colombian authorities of abetting the guerrillas, Castro denied having furnished arms but not having provided military training.[258] Subsequently, Cuban Vice President Carlos Rafael Rodriguez in an interview with the German magazine, *Der Speigel,* explicitly acknowledged Cuba's training role. Colombian President Julio Cesar Turbay Ayala found Cuban "explanations insufficient and in no way satisfactory" and suspended diplomatic relations with Cuba on March 23.[259] Later Turbay Ayala recalled:

> When we found that Cuba, a country with which we had diplomatic relations, was using those relations to prepare a group of guerrillas to come and fight against the Government, it was a kind of Pearl Harbor for us.[260]

Since then, Colombia has strived to alert Latin American governments about the new Cuban policy of "disguised intervention." Colombian Foreign Minister Carlos Lemos Simmonds described this at the OAS meeting in December 1981:

> Intervention has become subtle, artful, very skillful. It consists in utilizing internal conflicts, stirring them up, heightening them to the maximum of tension through political movements and parties precisely designed for this end and, once a chronic climate of protest has been created, to recruit among the most fanatical partisans of the revolution, the youngest, the least mature, the most impatient, to convert them into the spearhead of intervention.[261]

Chile

The Cubans also have been active in training and uniting Chilean political organizations for armed struggle. After the fall of Allende, the pro-Castro MIR set up headquarters in Cuba where it rapidly became dependent on Soviet and

Cuban sustenance and gradually abandoned its anti-Soviet stance. Relations with the traditional pro-Soviet Chilean Communist Party, heretofore despised as the promulgator of the disastrous Soviet peaceful transition policy, slowly warmed. Throughout the 1970s, MIR received political training in Cuba and, beginning in 1979 with Havana's and Moscow's reconversion to armed struggle, extensive military training.[262] By this time too, MIR was recruiting Chilean exiles for training in Cuba where eventually, with Cuban help in transport and acquisition of false documents, they were sent on to Chile.

By late 1980 the Chilean People's Resistance Militia was claiming responsibility for bombings, bank robberies, and the burning of department stores and restaurants, as well as attacks on army garrisons. In July 1981 *Granma* celebrated a total of more than 150 successful "armed actions."[263] Meanwhile, in December 1980, Chilean Communist Party leader Luis Corvalan[264] held extensive conversations with Castro, and that month, during the Cuban Communist Party congress, announced his adoption of the new Soviet-Cuban policy of armed struggle. He also acceded to Soviet-Cuban wishes by uniting with MIR and other hitherto heterodoxical ultra left forces. Radio Moscow broadcast the Chilean Communist Party policy revision in Spanish to Latin America and publicized them in their overseas press.[265]

Venezuela

Cuba's hostility to the democratic Venezuelan government dates from the early 1960s, when its training and arming of Venezuelan guerrillas led directly to the imposition of diplomatic and economic sanctions by the OAS, precipitating a decade-long diplomatic rupture. In the late 1960s and early 1970s, relations between Venezuela and Cuba improved, and by 1974 the social democratic (Accion Democratica) government of Carlos Andres Perez had renewed diplomatic relations with Cuba. Under Andres Perez's administration, Caracas later cooperated with Havana in equipping the Sandinistas. Relations began to cool again in late 1979, when Havana refused to grant exit visas to 18 Cubans who had taken refuge in the Venezuelan embassy. They deteriorated further when the Venezuelan Supreme Court acquitted four men accused of participating in a terrorist attack on a Cuban airliner in 1976.

Cuba's overt support for the Guyanese position in the dispute over Essequibo brought Cuban-Venezuelan relations close to the breaking point. By May 9, 1981 *Granma* was branding Venezuela's claim to the Essequibo "anti-Cuban."[266]

The Latin American Response

Venezuelan Foreign Minister Jose Alberto Zambrano Velasco has said that "Cuban actions in Central America and the Caribbean region are part of the global strategy of the Soviet Union."[267] Alarmed by Soviet and Cuban efforts to penetrate the region and by the prospect of a superpower confrontation, Venezuela has sought to forge a common Latin American strategy against outside intervention, tightening diplomatic relations with Argentina, Brazil, and Mexico. Venezuela opposes increased U.S. military deployments in the Caribbean, which it prefers to convert into "a zone of peace, not a strategic target of big powers...."[268] With this goal, Venezuela has provided various forms of economic assistance to the Caribbean including oil on favorable credit terms. It has also helped in developing educational and infrastructural projects to the Caribbean nations and has sought to encourage democratic reforms in the region.

Colombia has expressed its hope that Venezuela will

join its efforts to form a Latin American democratic front against Cuban adventurism.[269] Colombia has provided $10 million in bank loans and export credits to the new anti-Castro government in Jamaica and has signed an agreement with Chile "to combat Cuban expansionism."[270]

The Caribbean countries have also reacted against Soviet-Cuban expansionism. Cuba's sympathizers among the Surinam sergeants who seized power in February 1980 were later unseated. Cuban expansionism was a major issue in a recent series of electoral setbacks for Cuban supporters in Antigua, St. Vincent, Dominica, St. Lucia, St. Kitts-Nevis, and Jamaica. Newly-elected Jamaican Prime Minister Edward Seaga asked Cuba to recall its ambassador, Ulises Estrada, whom they accused of running covert activities on the island, and suspended technical agreements with Cuba. On January 29, 1981, Seaga told the Jamaican parliament that continued Cuban interference in Jamaican affairs left him with no choice but to sever diplomatic relations with Cuba.[271]

The social democratic regime in Santo Domingo has become concerned with Soviet-Cuban subversion, as we indicated in the previous chapter. It has retaliated by preventing Cuban sports delegations from entering the country to participate in regional sports competitions stating that "various Cuban police agents were detected" among them.[272] Widespread resistance in the Caribbean, certainly encouraged by the Reagan administration but caused not by the United States but by the fears of the Caribbean countries themselves, has forced Cuba into a somewhat lower profile in the region.

Panama

These fears are by no means confined to Caribbean counties. The evolution in Panama's relations with the Soviet Union and Cuba are an interesting example of the new trend. In the early 1970s the USSR, echoed by Cuba, was including Panama in its list of progressive military regimes. Articles in the Soviet press and statements in the United Nations in support of Panama in the Canal negotiations reflected the Soviet appreciation of the Canal's strategic importance.[273] The USSR attributed Panama's firm position to the new global correlation of forces and claimed credit for the convocation of the UN General Assembly in Panama in 1973.

Since 1974 the pro-Soviet People's Party of Panama has been a consistent supporter of the Panamanian military government. It secured important posts in the state bureaucracy, especially in the ministries of labor, education, transportation, and justice. Panama renewed diplomatic relations with Cuba in late 1974. The warm ties that developed between Castro and General Omar Torrijos owed more to personal than ideological affinity or shared views on the United States. In part the renewal of relations with Cuba was a calculation on Torrijos's part that this would pressure the United States to accelerate the negotiations.[274] The Cuban presence in Panama grew from four persons in 1975 to what became the second largest diplomatic mission in the country by the late 1970s. Frequent daily flights to and from Cuba and multiple cultural exchanges and tours have been organized. Scores of Panamanian students study in Cuba, and Cuban and Soviet literature is readily available in Panamanian bookstores. Torrijos cooperated with Castro in dispatching military equipment to the Sandinistas, and Panama sent doctors as well as military and diplomatic advisers to assist the new Nicaraguan government.

This picture began to change in 1979. Panamanian advisers returning from Nicaragua reported growing Cuban involvement in Nicaraguan internal affairs. Torrijos began to reevaluate his support for the Sandinista regime and for the FMLN. In October 1979 Panamanian teachers, students, and labor and peasant organizations staged a massive strike against the Ministry of Education's proposal to introduce Cuban textbooks, methods, and advisers into the Panamanian educational system.[275] This strike, which also included other demands, was the largest in Panama's history and forced the government to drop the plan and to reconsider other measures such as a pending commercial agreement with the USSR. Torrijos began to speak out against the Cuban position in the nonaligned movement and to condemn the Soviet invasion of Afghanistan; Panama then boycotted the Moscow Summer Olympics.[276] Increasingly worried about Cuban involvement in El Salvador, Torrijos also became disillusioned with the prospects for a negotiated settlement in that country. In an article in the Panamanian newspaper, *La Republica*, in the spring of 1981, shortly before he died in an airplane crash in the summer of 1981, he blasted Cuba for its interference in Central America.[277]

In the light of Torrijo's political evolution, it is interesting to note the Soviet-Cuban-Nicaraguan propaganda efforts to tie Torrijo's death to the CIA. The campaign, as is customary, began in *Pravda:*

> in planning the physical removal of Omar Torrijos, the US espionage agency fulfilled the orders of the American monopolies and the Pentagon who were dissatisfied with the progressive course of the Panamanian government.[278]

Similar accusations then appeared in *Granma*, in Nicaragua's *Barricada* and *Nuevo Diario*, and in pro-Soviet publications elsewhere in Latin America and around the world. No mention, of course, was made of Torrijos's recently changed views on Cuba and the Soviet Union, of his cooperation with the United States in Central America, and of his fears of Soviet-Cuban expansionism in the region.

Although the new government headed by Aristides Royo has proven to be, according to the pro-Soviet People's Party, "more progressive than its predecessor," it has generally followed Torrijos' policies.[279] The Royo government is cooperating with neighboring countries against Cuban interference in their internal affairs. After five Panamanian students were captured and jailed by Colombian authorities for their participation in arms traffic for the M-19, Panama's vice foreign minister went to Colombia to sign an agreement tightening border controls.[280]

Costa Rica

Cuba's relations with Costa Rica have also soured. The Costa Ricans have accused the USSR of interfering in local labor problems and abrogated a technical and economic agreement providing labor training by Soviet experts.[281] The government has also been embarrassed by the subsequent evolution of the Nicaraguan government after having sent arms to the Sandinistas. The strain in relations was compounded by an offensive comment made by a Cuban representative at the United Nations, attacking Costa Rica's position on the violations of human rights in Cuban jails.[282] On May 11, 1981, Costa Rica broke consular relations with Cuba.

Ecuador and Peru

A similar deterioration has occurred in relations with Ecuador and Peru as a result of Cuban violations of international norms at the time of the Cuban refugee exodus to the United States. Cuban strong-arm tactics in the Ecuadorian embassy in Havana in February 1980 led to the withdrawal

En Paita: Lluvias por encargo
("The rains we prayed for")

A 1977 Peruvian newspaper cartoon depicting Cuban troops in high spirits at Paita.

of the Ecuadorian ambassador on February 29, 1980. The Peruvian ambassador was recalled in April 1980 because of a Havana-sponsored invasion of its embassy "and the verbal violence of the Cuban communiqué" that followed.[283]

As a result of all of these developments, Cuba's diplomatic relations with Latin America have been virtually reduced to Argentina, Brazil, Mexico, Grenada, Guyana, and Panama. This is a dramatic deterioration from the situation of only a few years ago. Yet it is further evidence of the results of a basic change in the Soviet-Cuban orientation in which peaceful transition and the pursuit of normal diplomatic and commercial relations has been replaced with a policy of interference in the domestic affairs of Latin American countries.

For the most part the region's resistance to Soviet-Cuban expansionism is not ideological but political—it is opposition not to socialism but to outside interference in domestic affairs. As the minister of home affairs in Dominica explained in rejecting an offer of scholarships for Dominican students to study in Cuba,

> This government has no objection to any citizen of Dominica studying Marxism. We hold no objection to citizens of Dominica studying about the ideology of their choice. What we do object to is people forcing others to accept their ideology. . . .[284]

In other words, Dominica, like many other countries in the region, has "no quarrel with Cuba, unless Cuba intends to undermine the sovereignty of the country."[285]

These statements exemplify an often misunderstood aspect of Third World resistance to Soviet expansionism. Taken as a whole, this resistance is not to Marxism or to socialism per se, but to encroachments on national sovereignty. Yugoslavia's firm opposition to Cuba's attempt to align the nonaligned movement with Moscow, China's outspoken criticisms of Soviet hegemonism, Somalia's and Zimbabwe's alarm about Soviet expansionism in Africa, and the rising concern in the Socialist International, especially in the Costa Rican, Dominican, and Venezuelan parties, illustrate this. In general, the Third World does not accept the thesis that the main contradiction in the world is between the capitalist and socialist "camps."

For the countries of the south, the main enemy is neither capitalism nor socialism, but northern domination and intervention. In Latin America's own quest for independence lies the key to opposing Soviet hegemonism. Will the United States be capable of abandoning its own hegemonistic habits and supporting Latin America's aspirations? That is the big question for U.S. policy in Latin America.

9

Conclusion: Mutual Benefit, Mutual Defense

The preceding examination of Soviet activities has concentrated mainly on the central salient of Soviet penetration, the Caribbean Basin, and has paid little attention to another center of Soviet interest: the southern cone and the South Atlantic.

The Southern Cone

In the southern cone Moscow continues to favor peaceful penetration. In 1981 the USSR sharply expanded trade with Brazil and signed several scientific-technical agreements with that country. Since the early 1970s the Soviet Union has been the chief importer of Argentine grain and meat. Carefully cultivated relations with Argentine growers and exporters now supplement those with influential financial groups, small and medium-size industrialists, administrators of state companies, military officers, and government officials. According to Soviet officials, Argentina is now the USSR's most important grain seller, while the

Soviet market has become indispensable for Argentina.[286]
The Soviets participate as suppliers of turbines and genera-
tors in several important power projects in Argentina and
provide the Argentine nuclear program, the most advanced
in Latin America, with critical components such as enriched
uranium and heavy water.[287] In the past several years there
have been frequent exchanges of military missions between
Moscow and Buenos Aires, and high Argentine army officials have trained at the Leningrad military college. At the
moment in which Argentina's border conflict with Chile
reached the brink of war in 1978, occasioning the largest
military mobilization in the region in 40 years, the Soviet
army chose to decorate Lt. General Roberto Viola, the Argentine commander in chief, and *Red Star* declared support
for Argentina in the event of armed conflict with Chile.

The Soviets poured $650 million worth of military
equipment into Peru in the mid-1970s, including tanks,
supersonic fighter planes, heavy artillery, and the region's
first surface-to-air missiles. Moscow still retains considerable influence within the Peruvian military establishment.
In September of 1981 the Peruvian armed forces sought
governmental permission to purchase $200 million worth of
new equipment from the Soviets.[288]

Conclusions

A study of Soviet Latin American policy would examine in
detail Soviet relations with the southern cone as well as developing Soviet-Cuban commercial and diplomatic relations
with Mexico, which has become an important base for Soviet and Cuban cultural and propaganda efforts. But this
paper seeks only to draw attention to the shift in Soviet
strategy and tactics and to suggest a general policy response.

The main points of the argument can be summarized as follows:

(1) The intervention in Angola marked the beginning of a Soviet global, strategic offensive.

(2) Between 1968 and 1975 Cuba capitulated economically, politically, and ideologically to the Soviet superpower. Cuban prestige in the Third World and Cuban combatants, equipped by Moscow and under Soviet command, were put in the service of Moscow's African strategy. The role of Cuba is crucial to Soviet Latin American strategy.

(3) The Soviet global offensive was extended to Latin America when Central American revolutionary movements created propitious conditions.

(4) The geopolitical center of gravity of Soviet Latin American strategy has shifted from tactics of peaceful transition in the southern cone to those of armed struggle in the Caribbean Basin.

(5) The revolutionary process in Central America was not created in Moscow. The Soviets seek—via Cuba—to dominate the region and have had some success to date in Nicaragua, though less in El Salvador and Guatemala. Insofar as Central American revolutionary movements remain true to their primary purpose—national self-determination—the Soviets will encounter resistance in their efforts to bring them under control. But if these revolutions betray that aspiration, the revolutions themselves will encounter popular resistance.

(6) Resistance to Soviet-Cuban intervention has been growing in neighboring Latin American governments. This is an essential component of any anti-Soviet strategy in Latin America. The reaction against Soviet hegemonism, however, is not a call for renewed U.S. intervention or for any return to U.S. hegemony.

(7) The underlying principle of anti-Soviet resistance is not support for the United States or Western values, it is

nonintervention. Elements of a strategic consensus on Soviet expansion exist in Latin America, but fears of renewed U.S. hegemonism under President Reagan have impeded progress toward collective security. The Soviets' greatest strategic asset in Latin America, even greater than Cuba, is anti-Yankee sentiment, a result of a history of U.S. intervention in the region.

(8) As in the 1930s when another power sought world dominance, the United States must recognize once again the strategic imperative of a Good Neighbor policy. A Good Neighbor policy today must proceed from changed Latin American realities, especially its increased economic and political independence.

(9) A successful U.S. policy must include relations of mutual economic benefit, an even-handed human rights policy that exempts neither allies nor adversaries, military cooperation against external threats to national sovereignty but not against internal popular opposition, and extensive political consultation and coordination.[289] It is obviously in the U.S. interest to have friendly neighbors.

(10) The prospect of new Soviet bases in the Western hemisphere should be of concern to the United States because they would endanger the political independence of Latin America and the logistical support system of the Western alliance. To meet this challenge, the United States must learn to listen carefully to Latin Americans and develop a policy that takes into account local and regional as well as global realities.

The United States must recognize that the Third World has emerged as an independent strategic factor. The Soviet threat to the independence and peace of Third World countries has created common interests with Europe, Japan, Canada, Australia, and the United States. But U.S. actions perceived as unilateral, interventionist, or hegemonist will cloud Third World perceptions of the new Soviet danger. On the other hand, Western trade and technology can promote economic and political cooperation with the Third World.

U.S. behavior in its Latin American backyard is an index of our ability to live as good neighbors with Third World nations. The reputation of the United States in the Third World is of pressing strategic concern. In the coming years, U.S. ability to manage its relations with Latin America will play a major role in the outcome of the Soviet worldwide offensive.

Notes

1. Abraham F. Lowenthal, "The United States and Latin America: Ending the Hegemonic Presumption," *Foreign Affairs* 55 (October 1976):199-207.

2. *United Nations Commission on Trade and Development,* UNCTAD TD/243, Supplement 2:14.

3. V. Rogov in *Strany SEV i Latinskaya Amerika: Problemy ekonomicheskogo sotrudnichestva,* (Moscow: Nauka, 1976), p. 16, cited in *International Affairs* 7 (July 1976):126.

4. Y. Zhuravliov, "American Latina y el CAME: Tendencia en Las Relaciones," *America Latina* 4 (1976):8; *see also* P. Ananiev et al., *Economica de los Latinoamericanos* (Moscow: Progress, 1978), p. 493; T. Shugayev, "The USSR and Developing Countries," *International Affairs* 11 (Moscow, November 1979):119.

5. A Sizonenko, *Sovietskii Soyuz i Latinskaya Amerika,* (Kiev, 1976), pp. 19-20; XXV Congress of the Communist Party of the Soviet Union, "Guidelines for the Development of the USSR for 1976-1980," in *Strany Sotsialisticheskoi orientatsii: Osnovnye Tendentsii Razvitiya,* ed., N. A. Simoniya, 1976, p. 64.

6. Y. Zhuravliov, "America Latina," p. 8.

7. "On the Restructuring of International Economic Relations," *Pravda,* (October 5, 1976), p. 4.

8. G. B. Khromushin et al., *The Role of the State in Socio-*

Economic Reforms in Developing Countries (Moscow: Progress, 1976), p. 234.

9. U. S. Congress, Library of Congress, Congressional Research Service, *The Soviet Union and the Third World: A Watershed in Great Power Policy,* Report to the Committee on International Relations, U.S. House of Representatives, May 8, 1977, p. 114.

10. James R. Carter, *The Net Cost of Soviet Foreign Aid* (New York: Praeger, 1969), pp. 37–41.

11. See N. S. Patolichev (Soviet Foreign Trade Minister) in *Foreign Trade* (Moscow, 1976), p. 40; S. I. Tiul'panov, *Ocherki politcheskoi ekonomiki (Razvivanishchiesia strany)* (Moscow, 1969), p. 169–170 especially; J. Rudinski, "Mutual Benefits Derived from Socialist Cooperation," *Voprosy Economiki* 2 (Moscow, 1961); Morris Bernstein, "The Reform and Revaluation of the Ruble," *American Economic Review* (March 1961); cf. Franklin D. Holzman, *International Trade Under Communism* (New York: Basic Books, 1976), pp. 28, 101.

12. J. R. Carter, *Soviet Foreign Aid,* pp. 37–41.

13. Alexander Wolynski, "Soviet Aid to the Third World," *Conflict Studies* 90 (December 1977):4.

14. UNCTAD TD/243, Supplement 1, p. 24 (Table 10).

15. "Changing Patterns in Soviet-LDC Trade, 1976-7," Fig. 2, p. 3 (based on Soviet Foreign Trade Yearbooks), Central Intelligence Agency (CIA), May 1978. For an earlier tabulation with similar findings for the CMEA countries, see *Statistical Review of Trade between Countries having different Social and Economic Systems,* UNCTAD, TC/B/410 (Geneva, 1972):9, and for the USSR, R. Mukherji, *Economies of Soviet Aid and Trade* (Calcutta, 1978), Table 4, pp. 9–10, based on *Foreign Trade of the USSR for 1970* (Moscow, 1971).

16. Toby Trister Gati, "The Soviet Union and the North-South Dialogue," *Orbis* (Summer 1980), p. 256; Holzman, *International Trade,* p. 154, 178; J. S. Prybyla, "The Sino-Soviet Split and the Developing Nations," in *The Soviet Union and the Developing Nations,* ed., Roger E. Kanet (Baltimore: Johns Hopkins University Press, 1974), pp. 282–283; Kurt Muller, *The Foreign Aid Programs of the Soviet Bloc and China* (New York: Praeger, 1968), p. 210; U.S. Congress, Joint Economic Committee, "Sovi-

et Foreign Aid: Scope, Directions and Trends," in *Soviet Economic Prospects for the Seventies* (Washington, D.C., 1973), pp. 769–770.

17. U.S. Congress, Joint Economic Committee, "Soviet Economic Aid to the Third World," in *Soviet Economy in a New Perspective* (Washington, D.C., October 1976), pp. 193, 196; Alexander Wolynski, "Soviet Aid to the Third World," *Conflict Studies* 90 (December 1977):6.

18. As estimated by M. Kidion, *Foreign Investments* (London: Oxford University Press, 1965), p. 123; R. Mukherji, *Economics of Soviet Aid and Trade* (Calcutta, 1978), p. 171.

19. A. Grigoryev, "USSR-FRG: Economic Relations," *International Affairs* 10 (Moscow, October 1974):51.

20. A. M. Smirnov, *International Currency and Credit Relations* (Moscow, 1960), p. 275, cited in Mukherji, *Soviet Aid and Trade*, p. 189.

21. "Cuba's dependence on the USSR in carrying out military and security operations in Africa was first demonstrated during the Angolan crisis of 1975–76. The view that the Soviet role was confined primarily to the supply of weaponry is not correct. It is true that because of initial uncertainty regarding the American response, the Soviets were cautious about committing themselves in direct military fashion in Angola. Nevertheless, in early November 1975 they took over the air- and sea-lift, transforming the Angolan campaign into a massive operation during which both the Soviet Air Force and the Soviet Navy were operationally effective. A Soviet naval task force provided physical and psychological support to the Cuban combat troops, protected the Cuban staging areas against local threats, served as a strategic cover for established Cuban and Soviet sea and air communications, and worked as a deterrent against possible U.S. naval deployment." See Jiri Valenta, "The Soviet-Cuban Alliance in Africa," *Cuban Studies* XIX (July 1980):36–43; "The Soviet-Cuban Intervention in Angola, 1975," *Studies in Comparative Communism* (Spring/Summer 1978):3–33.

22. M. Maksimova, "The World Economy, The Scientific and Technological Revolution and International Relations," *Mirovaya Ekonomika i Mezhdunarodnye Otnosheniya* 4 (April 1979):23–33.

23. Derek D. Davies, "Moscow Meets the Dahlaks," *Far*

Eastern Economic Review (January 9, 1981), p. 14.

24. Nikita Khrushchev, "Speech at the UN General Assembly," October, 1960.

25. Nikita Khrushchev, "Report to the Session of the Supreme Court of the USSR," October, 1959.

26. "To the Detriment of the Struggle of the People," *Pravda,* September 17, 1963.

27. Central Committee of the Communist Party of the Soviet Union (CPSU), "Open Letter to All Party Organizations," July 14, 1963, part IV.

28. N. Khrushchev, "Vital Questions of the Development of the Socialist World System," *World Marxist Review* 9 (1962):18–19.

29. Central Committee of the CPSU, "Open Letter."

30. Leon Gouré and Morris Rothenberg, *Soviet Penetration of Latin America,* Institute for Advanced International Studies (IAIS) (Coral Gables: University of Miami Press, 1975), p. 133.

31. V. Vasileyev, "The US's 'New Approach' to Latin America," *International Affairs* 6 (Moscow, June 1971):48.

32. Alexandr Sizonenko, "Con Motivo Del XXVI Congreso Del PCUS:URSS-Paises Latinoamericanos: Resultados y Perspectivas de las Relaciones Interestatales," *America Latina* 1–2 (1981): 14.

33. G. Fichet, "Tres decenios de relaciones entre America Latina y la Union Sovietica," *Comercio Exterior* 2, vol. 31 (Mexico, February 1981):165–166.

34. Cole Blasier, "Soviet Relations with Latin America in the 1970s," (Washington, D.C.: The National Council for Soviet and East European Research, 1980):III 6, 9.

35. Calculated from CIA (1978), *Communist Aid to the Less Developed Countries,* p. 6; CIA, "Communist States and Developing Countries, Aid and Trade in 1973," October 1974, as cited in Gouré and Rothenberg, *Soviet Penetration of Latin America,* pp. 135–136.

36. CIA, "Communist States and Developing Countries: Aid and Trade in 1974," January 1976, p. 4.

37. UNCTAD, TD/243, Supplement 2, Manila, May 1979, p. 28.

38. N. Gladkov, "Trade and Economic Relations Between the Soviet Union and the Developing Latin American Countries," *Foreign Trade* 12 (Moscow, 1975):12. See UNCTAD V, "Tripartite Industrial Cooperation and Cooperation in Third Countries." TD/243, Supplement 5, Manila, 1979.

39. Y. Zhuravliov, "America Latina y el CAME Tendencia en las Relaciones," *America Latina* 4 (1976):13.

40. Gouré and Rothenberg, *Soviet Penetration*, p. 165.

41. Victor Volskii, et al., *SSSR i Latinskaya Amerika, 1917-1967,* (Moscow: Izdatel'stvo Mezhdunarodnyee Otnosheniya 1967), p. 123.

42. Sizonenko, "Con Motivo Del XXVI Congreso," p. 16; Gouré and Rothenberg, *Soviet Penetration*, pp. 170-171.

43. C. Tarasov, *SShA i Latinskaya Amerika* (Moscow: Polizdat, 1972), p. 29; Vasilyev, "The US's 'New Approach,' " p. 43; S. Mishin, "Latin America: Two Trends of Development," *International Affairs* (Moscow, June 1976):54-61.

44. *Granma Weekly Review*, August 20, 1967.

45. G. Karstag, "Concerning the Development of the Revolutionary Process in Latin America," *Latinskaya Amerika* 1 (Moscow, January-February 1972), Joint Publications Research Service (JPRS) Translation, p. 71.

46. *Pravda*, July 30, 1967.

47. G. Karstag, "Revolutionary Process in Latin America," p. 70.

48. Ibid., p. 74.

49. Ibid., p. 77.

50. L. Brezhnev, "Report of the Central Committee of the Communist Party of the Soviet Union" (Novosti, 1971), p. 25; Boris Ponomarev, "Topical Problems of the Theory of the Revolutionary Process," *Kommunist* (October 1971); JPRS 54571, 1971, p. 72.

51. Ponomarev, "Topical Problems," p. 73.

52. Ibid.

53. Victor Volskii, "The Problems of the Peaceful Path to Socialism," *America Latina* 3 (1974):21.

54. Ponomarev, "Topical Problems," p. 74.

55. J. Kobo, "Concerning Some Peculiarities of the Evolu-

tion of the Armies of the Latin American Continent," *Latinskaya Amerika* 4 (1971):52.

56. Ponomarev, "Topical Problems," p. 75.

57. Ibid.

58. Ibid., p. 74.

59. V. Bushuyev, "New Trends in Latin American Armed Forces," *Krasnaya Zvezda* (October 3, 1972) in JPRS-Latin America 881 (October 26, 1972):4.

60. Ibid.

61. Ibid., p. 5.

62. Ibid., p. 3.

63. Ibid., p. 4.

64. Ibid., p. 5.

65. Ponomarev, "Topical Problems," p. 74.

66. Ibid.

67. V. I. Lenin, *Lenin Selected Works,* Vol. III (Moscow) p. 327.

68. James D. Theberge, "Soviet Relations with Allende's Chile and Valasco's Peru," Monograph (Washington, D.C.: Center for Strategic and International Studies [CSIS], Georgetown University, August 1974), p. 20.

69. V. Morozov, *International Economic Organization of the Socialist States* (Moscow: Novosti, 1973), p. 15.

70. Oscar Arevalo, "Reactionary Intrigues Notwithstanding," interview in *New Times* 31 (Moscow, July 1977):11.

71. Rodolfo Ghioldi, "Algunos Problemas de la Etapa Contemporanea del Desarrollo de Paises de America Latina," *America Latina* 2 (1979):50.

72. *New Times* 51 (Moscow, December 1977):51.

73. Arevalo, "Reactionary Intrigues," p. 11.

74. Karen N. Brutents, *National Liberation Revolutions Today* I (Moscow: Progress, 1977): 16. See Morris Rothenberg, *The USSR and Africa: New Dimensions of Soviet Global Power* (Coral Gables: IAIS, 1980), p. 257.

75. N. I. Gavtilov and G. B. Starushenko, eds., *Africa: Problems of Socialist Orientation* (Moscow: Nauka, 1976), pp. 10–11.

76. Jiri Valenta, "The USSR, Cuba and the Crisis in Central America," *ORBIS,* Fall 1981, p. 736.

77. Nikolai Leonov, "Nicaragua: Experiencia de una Revolucion Victoriosa," *America Latina* 3 (1980):37.

78. Sergei Mikoyan, "Las Particularidades de la Revolucion en Nicaragua y sus Tareas desde el punto de vista de la Teoria y la Practica de Movimiento Liberador," *America Latina* 3 (1980): 101.

79. Boris Koval, "La Revolucion, Largo Proceso Historico," *America Latina* 3 (1980):78.

80. N. Leonov, "Nicaragua," p. 37.

81. S. Mikoyan, "La Revolucion en Nicaragua," pp. 102–103.

82. Y. Korolev, "The Timeliness of the Chilean Experience," *Latinskaya Amerika* (September 1980), p. 9.

83. See "Discurso de Louis Corvalan Con Motivo del 10° Aniversario del Triunfo de la Unidad Popular," *America Latina* 10 (1980).

84. Luis Corvalan, "Discurso de Luis Corvalan Con Motivo del 10° Aniversario del Triunfo de la Unidad Popular" (Pronunciado el 3 de Septiembre de 1980), *America Latina* 10 (November 1980):111.

85. Rodney Arismendi, quoted in Alexander Sukhostat et al., "A Continent in Struggle," *World Marxist Review* (June 1981): p. 47.

86. Arnoldo Ferreto, "Revolution: The Ways to do it," *World Marxist Review* (October 1979), p. 63; Milton Rene Paredes, "Central America: The Masses are Beginning to Act," *World Marxist Review* (May 1980), p. 41; Carlos Gonzales, "Revolution: The Ways to It," *World Marxist Review* (October 1979), p. 58.

87. Shafik Jorge Handal, "Na Putik Svobode" ("On the Road to Freedom"), *Kommunist* 17 (November 1980):103.

88. Ramirez, "Nicaragua: from Armed Struggle to Construction," *World Marxist Review* (January 1980), p. 52.

89. Boris Koval, "La Revolucion, Largo Proceso Historico," *America Latina* 3 (1980):76–79; Sergei Mikoyan, "La Creatividad Revolucionaria Abre el Camino hacia la Victoria," *America Latina* 2 (1980):5; B. Koval, "La Revolucion," p. 78.

90. Sukhostat et al., "A Continent in Struggle," p. 47; Antonio Castro, "A Step Toward Unity," *World Marxist Review* (March 1981), p. 68.

91. S. Mikoyan, "La Revolucion en Nicaragua," p. 104; B. Koval, "La Revolucion," pp. 79–80.

92. S. Mikoyan, "La Revolucion en Nicaragua," pp. 105–106.

93. Kiva Maidanik, "La Unidad: Un Problema Clave," *America Latina* 3 (1980):44.

94. Alexander Morejin and Vladimir Tsaregovodtsev, "En lucha por los Intereses del Pueblo," *America Latina* 4 (1979):166.

95. I. Bulychev, "Nikaragua: Na Putakh Stroitel'stva Novoi Zhizhni" ("Nicaragua: On the Road to Building a New Life"); *Mirovaya Ekonomika i Mezhdunarodnye Otnosheniya* (December 1980), p. 81.

96. K. Maidanik, "La Unidad," p. 44.

97. A. Castro, "A Step Toward Unity," p. 68.

98. Eduardo Mora Valverde, "Costa Rica: Conditions for Revolution," *World Marxist Review* (October 1980), pp. 23–24.

99. Pedro Antonio Saad, "Our Arms and our Course," *World Marxist Review* (March 1980), p. 44.

100. Gabor Karstag, "Concerning the Development of the Revolutionary Process in Latin America," *Latinskaya Amerika* 1 (January-February 1972):77.

101. K. Brutents, *National Liberation Revolutions Today*, Vol. II, p. 217; M. Rothenberg, *The USSR and Africa*, p. 217.

102. R. Wyanovsky, "O Stranakh Sotsialisticheskoy Orientatsii" ("On the Countries of Socialist Orientation"), *Kommunist* 11 (July 1979):119.

103. Boris Ponomarev, "The Cause of Freedom and Socialism is Invincible," *World Marxist Review* (January 1981), p. 13.

104. R. Wyanovsky, "Countries of Socialist Orientation," p. 118.

105. Boris Ponomarev, "Sovmestnaya Bor'ba rabochevo i natsional'no-osvobozhditel'nogo dvizhenii protiv imperialisma, za sotsial'nii progress" ("Joint struggle of the Labor and National Liberation Movements against Imperialism, for Social Progress"), *Kommunist* 16 (November 1980):41.

106. B. Ponomarev, "The Cause of Freedom and Socialism," p. 13.

107. M. Rothenberg, *The USSR and Africa*, p. 104.

108. I. Agayev and Tatarovskaia, "Some Problems in the

Development of the Revolutionary Process in Liberated Countries," *The Working Class and the Contemporary World* 5 (September–October 1976):57.

109. TASS, October 13, 1976, quoted in M. Rothenberg, *The USSR and Africa*, p. 122.

110. Ilya Bimov, "El Frente Sandinista de Liberacion Nacional, Fuerza Decisiva en la Lucha," *America Latina* 3 (1980):32.

111. M. S. Chumakova, "Nicaragua Viewed One Year After the Revolution," *Latinskaya Amerika* (July 1980), 26 (JPRS 76700, October 27, 1980, p. 32).

112. *Pravda*, "Joint Soviet-Nicaraguan Communique," March 23, 1980, p. 4.

113. S. Mikoyan, "La Revolucion en Nicaragua," pp. 110–111.

114. Ibid., p. 112.

115. Ibid., pp. 113–114.

116. R. Arismendi, "A Continent in Struggle," p. 47.

117. Ibid.

118. S. Mikoyan, "La Revolucion en Nicaragua," p. 106. See K. Maidanik, "La Unidad," pp. 44–45.

119. K. Maidanik, "La Unidad," p. 44.

120. S. Mikoyan, "La Revolution en Nicaragua," p. 102.

121. N. Leonov, "Nicaragua," p. 37.

122. Maurice Halperin, *The Taming of Fidel Castro* (Berkeley and London: University of California Press, 1981).

123. *Politica Internacional* 9, 1st trimestre (1965):238. See M. Halperin, *The Taming of Fidel Castro*, p. 126.

124. Jacques Levesque, *The USSR and the Cuban Revolution* (New York: Praeger, 1978), p. 110; D. Bruce Jackson, *Castro, the Kremlin, and Communism in Latin America* (Baltimore: Johns Hopkins Press, 1969), pp. 34–35.

125. Fidel Castro, "Speech of March 13, 1965," *Pravda*, March 19, 1965, quoted in J. Levesque, *The USSR and the Cuban Revolution*, p. 111.

126. William E. Ratliff, *Castroism and Communism in Latin America, 1959-1976* (Washington, D.C.: American Enterprise Institute (AEI)-Hoover Policy Study 19, November 1976), p. 44.

127. J. Levesque, *The USSR and the Cuban Revolution*, p. 148.

128. *Ogonek* 21 (June 1970):3, cited in Gouré and Rothen-

berg, *Soviet Penetration of Latin America,* p. 50.

129. Jorge I. Dominguez, *Cuba: Order and Revolution* (Cambridge, Mass.: Harvard University Press, 1978), p. 159; Carmelo Mesa-Lago, *Cuba in the 1970s: Pragmatism and Institutionalization* (Albuquerque: University of New Mexico Press, 1978), p. 10.

130. L. Gouré and M. Rothenberg, *Soviet Penetration of Latin America,* p. 54.

131. Carmelo Mesa-Lago, *Cuba in the 1970s,* pp. 17-18.

132. O. Galin, "The Cuban Communists in the Struggle for Socialism," *Partinaya Zhizn' Zhizni* 1 (January 1974):74; L. Gouré and M. Rothenberg, *Soviet Penetration of Latin America,* pp. 64-65; Morris Rothenberg, *Current Cuban-Soviet Relationships: The Challenge to U.S. Policy* (Coral Gables: Center for Advanced International Studies, University of Miami Press, 1974), pp. 7-8.

133. Robert Moss, "Soviet Ambitions in Latin America," in *The Southern Oceans and the Security of the Free World,* ed. Patrick Wall (London: Spacey International, 1977), p. 196.

134. Ibid., p. 195.

135. M. Rothenberg, *Cuban-Soviet Relationships,* pp. 8-9.

136. Carlos Alberto Montaner, *Secret Report on the Cuban Revolution* (New Brunswick, N.J.: Transaction Books, 1981), p. 42; J. Dominguez, *Cuba: Order and Revolution,* p. 160.

137. *Granma Weekly Review,* November 7, 1971, p. 1.

138. Ibid., January 9, 1972, p. 10; Carmelo Mesa-Lago, *Cuba in the 1970s,* p. 13.

139. Carmelo Mesa-Lago, *Cuba in the 1970s,* p. 16.

140. Fidel Castro, "Speech on the XIXth Anniversary of the Moncada Garrison," *Granma Weekly Review,* August 6, 1972, p. 3.

141. *Granma Weekly Review,* September 16, 1973.

142. Ibid.

143. M. Halperin, *The Taming of Fidel Castro,* p. 251.

144. Ibid., p. 252.

145. *Krasnaya Zvezda,* January 1, 1969, cited in Gouré and Rothenberg, *Soviet Penetration of Latin America,* p. 31.

146. *Krasnaya Zvezda,* December 2, 1969, cited in Gouré and Rothenberg, *Soviet Penetration of Latin America,* p. 31.

147. James D. Theberge, *Russia in the Caribbean,* Part 2,

(Washington, D.C.: CSIS, 1973), pp. 103-105, Table 7.

148. Christopher A. Abel, "A Breach in the Ramparts," *The Proceedings of the U.S. Naval Institute* (July 1980), p. 47; Barry Blechman and Stephanie Levinson, "Soviet Submarine Visits to Cuba," *The Proceedings of the U.S. Naval Institute* (September 1975), pp. 32-33; Captain Leslie K. Fenton, "The Umpteenth Cuban Confrontation," *The Proceedings of the U.S. Naval Institute* (July 1980), pp. 44.

149. C. Abel, "A Breach in the Ramparts," p. 47.

150. Ibid., p. 50; Micky Edwards, "Soviet Expansion and Control of the Sea Lanes," *The Proceedings of the U.S. Naval Institute* (September 1980), pp. 50-51.

151. Jorge I. Dominguez, "The United States and its Regional Security Interests: The Caribbean, Central and South America," *Daedalus* (Fall 1980), pp. 119-120.

152. Jiri Valenta, "Soviet Strategy in the Caribbean Basin," U.S. Naval Institute, *Proceedings*, May 1982, p. 172.

153. *Air Force Magazine* (December 1979), p. 118; *The Christian Science Monitor*, October 11, 1979, p. 9; David C. Jordan, "The Turbulent Caribbean," *Strategic Review* (Fall 1980), p. 42; *Baltimore Sun*, August 4, 1981, p. 4; *The Military Balance: 1981-1982* (London: International Institute for Strategic Studies [IISS], 1981), p. 96.

154. U.S., Department of State, Office of Cuban Affairs, Office of Inter-American Affairs, "Cuban Armed Forces and the Soviet Military Presence," 1981, p. 2.

155. Ibid., charts 2,3.

156. James D. Theberge, *Russia in the Caribbean*, p. 80.

157. *The Military Balance: 1981-1982*, p. 96.

158. Stockholm International Peace Research Institute (SIPRI), *SIPRI Yearbook: 1979* (Stockholm: SIPRI, 1979), pp. 210-211; *The Military Balance: 1979-1980* (London: IISS, 1979), p. 107; Carmelo Mesa-Lago, *Cuba in the 1970s*, p. 14.

159. *Strategic Survey: 1977* (London: IISS, 1978), p. 13.

160. William M. Leogrande, "Cuban Policy in Africa," *Cuban Studies* 10 (January 1980):21.

161. Jiri Valenta, "The USSR, Cuba and the Crisis in Central America," p. 730.

162. William M. Leogrande, "Cuban Dependency: A Comparison of Pre-Revolutionary and Post-Revolutionary International Economic Relations," *Cuban Studies* 2, vol. IX (July 1979): 3-22.

163. Conseil de l'Atlantique Nord/North Atlantic Council, "Soviet-Cuban Economic Relations," NATO Unclassified Document C-M (81) 34, May 15, 1981, Table II, Annex I.

164. Ibid., p. 23.

165. Larry Theriot, "Soviet Economic Relations with Non-European COMECON: Cuba, Vietnam, Mongolia," in *Soviet Economy in a Time of Change,* report to the Joint Economic Committee of the Congress (U.S. Department of Commerce, October 10, 1979), pp. 559-560; *Newsweek* (June 8, 1981), p. 62.

166. Larry Theriot and John Biggon, "Cuban Trade with CMEA, 1974-1979," East-West Trade Policy staff paper, International Trade Administration, U.S. Department of Commerce, April 1981; Fidel Castro speech, December 27, 1979, p. 34.

167. Havana Domestic Radio Service, April 21, 1981, from the Foreign Broadcast Information Service (FBIS), Latin America, April 21, 1981, Q9; November 3, 1980, Q1.

168. East-West Trade Policy Staff Paper, April 1981, pp. 8, 18.

169. Conseil de l'Atlantique Nord, "Soviet-Cuban Economic Relations," p. 24.

170. U.S., Department of State, "Cuba's Renewed Support for Violence in the Hemisphere," research paper presented to the Subcommittee on Western Hemispheric Affairs, Senate Foreign Relations Committee (Washington, D.C., December 14, 1981), pp. 1-12, Special Report No. 90.

171. Richard Sim and James Anderson, "The Caribbean Strategic Vacuum," *Conflict Studies* 121 (August 1980):2.

172. Robert S. Leiken, "The Author Replies," *Foreign Policy* 43 (Summer 1981):190.

173. U.S., Congress, House, Committee on Armed Services, Testimony of Admiral Thomas B. Hayward, chief of naval operations, "Report to the Subcommittee on Sea Power and Strategic and Critical Materials of the House Committee on Armed Services in Fiscal Year 1980 and 1981," *Military Posture,* Washington, D.C., 1980 and 1981, p. 4.

174. Peter G. Peterson, *The U.S. in the Changing World Economy* (Washington, D.C.: Government Printing Office, 1971), 2 volumes.

175. Paul Seidenman, "The Caribbean: A Sense of Urgency," *National Defense* (March 1981), p. 50; F. Clifton Berky, "Cuba's Expanding Power," *Air Force* (April 1980), p. 45-46.

176. Radio Paris, January 21, 1981, from FBIS, Latin America, January 21, 1981, p. 52.

177. Radio Managua, from FBIS, Latin America, March 30, 1981. See Jiri Valenta, "The USSR, Cuba and the Crisis in Central America," p. 34.

178. Harold W. Rood, *Kingdoms of the Blind* (Durham, N.C.: Carolina Academic Press, 1980), pp. 139-140.

179. Admiral A. T. Mahan, *The Interests of America in Sea Power, Present and Future* (Boston: Little Brown and Co., 1898), p. 289.

180. Sergei Gorshkov, *Naval Power in Soviet Policy*, (Moscow: Voenizdat, 1979), pp. 11-12.

181. Harold W. Rood, *Kingdoms of the Blind*, pp. 140-147.

182. Jiri Valenta, "The USSR, Cuba and the Crisis in Central America," p. 727.

183. Sergei Gorshkov, *The Sea Power of the State* (Elmsford, N.Y.: Pergamon, 1979), p. 252.

184. Anthony Maingot, "Cuba and the Commonwealth Caribbean: Playing the Cuban Card," *Caribbean Review* (Winter 1980), p. 44.

185. See Raymond Duncan, "Caribbean Leftism," *Problems of Communism* 27 (May-June 1978):35-37; R. Sim and J. Anderson, "The Caribbean Strategic Vacuum," p. 5.

186. R. Sim and J. Anderson, "The Caribbean Strategic Vacuum," p. 5.

187. "Cuba's Renewed Support for Violence," p. 9; *Conservative Digest* (September 1979), p. 33.

188. U.S. Department of State, "Cuba's Support for Violence," p. 9.

189. Ibid.

190. Anthony Maingot in *Caribbean Review* (Winter 1980), p. 44.

191. *Diario Las Americas*, July 22, 1981, p. 11.

192. U.S., Department of State, "Cuba's Renewed Support for Violence," p. 10; *Diario Las Americas,* April 22, 1981, p. 11.

193. *Diario Las Americas,* July 22, 1981, p. 11; FBIS, Latin America, September 24, 1981, p. S7; October 8, 1981, pp. 1–2.

194. FBIS, Latin America, November 12, 1981, p. S1.

195. "Jovenes de Grenada van a Cuba a Recibir la Educacion Socialista," *Diario Las Americas,* April 22, 1981, p. 11; Maxwell Marrow, "The Cuban Yoke," *National Review* (June 12, 1981): 666.

196. R. Sim and J. Anderson, "The Caribbean Strategic Vacuum," p. 4.

197. Vladimir Pavlovsky, "Flowers for the Legendary Cuffy," *New Times* 22 (May 1981):25.

198. Raymond Duncan, "Caribbean Leftism," *Problems of Communism* (May–June 1978), p. 48.

199. Donald Waters, "Jungle Politics: the People's Temple and the Affairs of State," *Caribbean Review* (Spring 1980).

200. cf. James Reston, Jr., *Our Father Who Art in Hell* (New York: Times Books, 1981), p. 168–204.

201. U.S. Department of State, "Cuba's Renewed Support for Violence," p. 9, *Diario Las Americas,* August 20, 1981, p. 11.

202. "Fear and Futility in Guyana," *The New Republic* (April 25, 1981), p. 18.

203. Vladimir Pavlovsky, "Flowers for the Legendary Cuffy," p. 26.

204. FBIS, Latin America, June 4, 1981, p. Q–4.

205. *Strategy Week,* July 20–26, 1981.

206. *Diario Las Americas,* July 21, 1981.

207. U.S., Department of State, "Cuba's Renewed Support for Violence," p. 10, *Diario Las Americas,* "Advierten sobre la Penetracion Roja en la Republica Dominicana," August 15, 1981.

208. U.S., Department of State, "Cuba's Renewed Support for Violence," p. 20; FBIS, Latin America, October 30, 1981, p. S–1.

209. William R. Cline and Enrique Delgado, eds., "Economic Integration in Central America," study sponsored jointly by the Brookings Institution and the Secretariat of Economic Integration of Central America (SEICA), (Washington, D.C.: Brook-

ings Institution, 1978), pp. 196, 198, 323–327; Richard Feinberg, "No Easy Answers," *Foreign Affairs* (Summer 1981), p. 1121; Isaac Cohen and Gert Rosenthal, "The International Aspects of the Crisis in Central America," prepared for a workshop on "The International Aspects of the Crisis in Central America," at the Woodrow Wilson International Center for Scholars, Washington, D.C., April 2–3, 1981.

210. SEICA, VI *Compendio Estadistico Centroamericano*, Guatemala, 1975; "Centroamerica: Estadisticas Macroeconomicas 1971–1975," SEICA/96/PES/8, June 1976; Monteforte Toledo Ms., *Centroamerica: Subdesarrollo y Dependencia* (Mexico: UNAM, 1972).

211. I. Cohen and G. Rosenthal, "The International Aspects of the Crisis in Central America."

212. Clark Reynolds, "Fissures in the Volcano? Central American Economic Prospects," in *Latin America and World Economy: A Changing International Order*, ed. Joseph Grunwald (Beverly Hills: Sage, 1981), vol. 2, p. 203.

213. Guillermo Molina Chocano, "Centroamerica: la crisis del viejo orden," cuadro 3.0 (Tegucigalpa, Honduras, 1981).

214. Brookings-SEICA, "Economic Integration in Central America," pp. 241–244.

215. Richard Feinberg, "No Easy Answers," p. 1137.

216. cf. Richard Millet, "Central American Paralysis," *Foreign Policy* (Summer 1980), p. 112.

217. "U.S. Policy for Nicaragua: No Force but Some Fleeing," *Miami Herald*, November 26, 1981.

218. U.S., Congress, House, Subcommittee on Inter-American Affairs, "Impact of Cuban-Soviet Ties in the Western Hemisphere," Hearings, 96th Cong., 1st, 2nd sess., April 25–26, 1979, p. 29; March 26–27, April 16–17, May 14, 1980, p. 17; Gilbert Lewthuaite, "Military Diplomatic Fronts Close in on Somoza," *Baltimore Sun*, June 19, 1979; *Diario Las Americas*, March 28, 1981, p. 10.

219. See CIA, "National Intelligence Estimate," May 2, 1979; Jiri Valenta, "The USSR, Cuba and the Crisis in Central America," p. 736.

220. International Bank for Reconstruction and Develop-

ment (IBRD), *World Development Report 1980* (New York: Oxford University Press, 1980), p. 112.

221. "A Revolutionary Friendship Turns Sour," *Latin America Weekly Report* WR-79-08 (December 21, 1979), p. 2; "Glacial Chill Settles Over Cuba's Ties with Latins," *Washington Post,* September 30, 1981; *New York Times,* September 9, 1981, p. E3.

222. See, *Status of U.S. Bilateral Relations with Countries of Latin America,* report of a study mission to Jamaica, Peru, Argentina, Costa Rica, and Brazil, January 8–17, 1981, submitted to the Committee on Foreign Affairs of the United States House of Representatives, p. 22. Carlos Andres Perez expressed his concerns on "Primer Plano," a Venezuelan television program, on February 2, 1982.

223. U.S., Department of State, *Communist Interference in El Salvador,* Special Report no. 80, February 23, 1981, Document 9; U.S., Department of State, "Cuba's Renewed Support for Violence," p. 3.

224. U.S., Department of State, *Communist Interference in El Salvador,* Document E, February 23, 1981.

225. Shafik Jorge Handal, "On the Road to Freedom."

226. Robert Rand, "The USSR's Stake in El Salvador," Radio Liberty Research, RL 126/81 (March 20, 1981), p. 3.

227. Shafik Jorge Handal, "On the Road to Freedom," p. 100.

228. U.S., Department of State, "Cuba's Renewed Support for Violence," p. 18.

229. Ibid., p. 19; *Daily Telegraph,* May 6, 1981; *Conservative Digest* (September 1979), p. 28.

230. U.S., Department of State, "Cuba's Renewed Support for Violence," p. 8.

231. Antonio Castro, interviewed in "A Step Toward Unity," *World Marxist Review,* March 1981, p. 68.

232. U.S., Department of State, "Cuba's Renewed Support for Violence," p. 22.

233. FBIS, Latin America, June 29, 1981, p. 4; *Diario Las Americas,* June 28, 1981; U.S., Department of State, "Cuba's Renewed Support for Violence," pp. 7–8.

234. Ibid., pp. 7-8, FBIS, Latin America, August 4, 1981, p. 8.

235. Ibid., pp. 7-8.

236. Ibid. Construction," *World Marxist Review* (January 1980), pp. 52-54; see R. Ulyanovsky, "O Stranakh Sotsialisticheskoi Orientatsii" ("On the Countries of Socialist Orientation"), *Kommunist* 11 (July 1979):114-123; Boris Ponomarev, "The Cause of Freedom and Socialism is Invincible," *World Marxist Review* (January 1981), pp. 17-19.

238. "U.S. and Soviet Competition in Arms Exports and Military Assistance," *Armed Forces International Journal*, part II (August 5, 1981):6-7.

239. *Latinskaya Amerika*, March 1980, p. 36.

240. "Haig Says U.S. 'Watching Flow of Arms to Nicaragua,'" *Washington Post*, June 3, 1981; *Wall Street Journal*, July 13, 1981, p. 12.

241. Interview with Enrique Dreyfus, chairman of the Superior Council of the Private Sector in Nicaragua, August 13, 1981.

242. N. I. Gavtilov and G. B. Starushenko, eds., *Africa: Problems of Socialist Orientation* (Moscow: Nauka, 1976), pp. 10-11.

243. See Robert S. Leiken, "Eastern Winds in Latin America," *Foreign Policy* 42 (Spring 1981):101.

244. See "Soviet Aid to Nicaragua Spurts," *Soviet World Outlook* 9 (September 1981):3.

245. Ibid.

246. Ibid.; *Diario Las Americas*, May 25, 1981; FBIS, Latin America, Radio Managua, June 8, 1981, p. 13; *The Miami Herald*, May 14, 1981.

247. "Boletin de Informacion de la Embajada de la URSS" (Mexico), April 1980, p. 3; Managua Radio Domestic Service, August 4, 1981, FBIS, Latin America, August 4, 1981, p. 20, July 30, 1981, p. 13; *Diario Las Americas*, August 6, 1981, p. 6; Christopher Dickey, "Arab States Help Nicaragua Avoid Ties to Superpowers," *Washington Post*, July 19, 1981.

248. *Diario Las Americas*, "2 Helicopteros Prestara Rusia a Nicaragua," April 25, 1981; *Diario Las Americas*, "Asesores Sovi-

eticos Adiestran a Sandinistas en Helicopteros," June 6, 1981; Ronald Richards, "Soviets 'hinted' copter training in Nicaragua," *Providence Journal,* June 9, 1981.

249. "Nicaraguans Said to Get Soviet Tanks," *Washington Post,* June 2, 1981, p. A1, 4, and p. A20; "Les pays arabes accroissent leur aide militaire au gouvernement sandiniste," *Le Monde,* July 21, 1981, p. 4; Juan Vasquez, "Nicaragua Confirms It Has Been Given Some Soviet Tanks," *Los Angeles Times,* July 15, 1981; "Les dirigeants nicaraguayens admettent avoir recu des chars sovietiques," *Le Monde,* July 17, 1981; "Tanques Rusos a Nicaragua," *Diario Las Americas,* July 16, 1981.

250. Managuan Radio, March 27, 1981, FBIS, Latin America, March 30, 1981 as cited in Jiri Valenta, "The USSR, Cuba and the Crisis in Central America," p. 738.

251. N. I. Gavtilov, G. B. Starushenko, eds., *Africa: Problems of Socialist Orientation,* pp. 10-11.

252. Charles A. Krause, "Nicaraguan Defense Minister Sets Off on Arms-Buying Trip," *Washington Post,* September 1, 1979.

253. Speech to Military Specialists by Humberto Ortega Saavedra, Commander of the Revolution, August 25, 1981.

254. *Boston Globe,* April 17, 1981, p. 2.

255. *Latin America Weekly Report* (July 31, 1981):4-5; U.S., Department of State, "Cuba's Renewed Support for Violence," p. 10.

256. Julio Scherer Garcia, interview with Fidel Castro: "No es ficcion," *Proceso* (September 14, 1981).

257. FBIS, Latin America, March 30, 1981, p. F-1, June 1, 1981, p. F-1; *Diario Las Americas,* March 27, 1981; U.S. Department of State, "Cuba's Renewed Support for Violence," p. 31.

258. *Diario Las Americas,* March 27, 1981.

259. FBIS, Latin America, March 27, 1981, p. F-2; *Diario Las Americas,* March 26, 1981.

260. *New York Times,* August 13, 1981, p. A3.

261. *Diario Las Americas,* December 6, 1981, p. 14-C.

262. U.S. Department of State, "Cuba's Renewed Support for Violence," p. 11.

263. *Granma,* February 8, 1981, p. 11, July 26, 1981, p. 15.

264. Corvalan was released from prison in December 1976

by the Pinochet government in exchange for Soviet dissident author Vladimir Bukowski. He took up residence in the Soviet Union and became the center of the worldwide Soviet-orchestrated campaign against the Chilean Junta.

265. U.S. Department of State, "Cuba's Renewed Support for Violence," p. 11.

266. FBIS, Latin America, May 11, 1981, p. Q-1.

267. *El Nacional* (Caracas), March 1, 1981.

268. See Venezuelan President Herrera Campins, "State of the Nation Speech," March, 1981.

269. FBIS, Latin America, April 9, 1981, p. F-1.

270. *New York Times,* August 13, 1981, p. A3.

271. *Washington Star,* January 28, 1981, p. A17; *Miami Herald,* October 30, 1981, p. 1.

272. FBIS, Latin America, August 11, 1981, p. Q-1; *Diario Las Americas,* July 21, 1981.

273. R. D. Souza, "Panama: New Perspectives of Struggle," *Latinskaya Amerika* 1 (Jan–Feb 1973):25.

274. See David Binder, "How to Deal with Gringos," *The New Republic* (February 14, 1976), p. 7–8.

275. *La Estrella de Panama,* October 10, 1979, p. 1.

276. See the *Washington Post,* October 2, 1980, p. 33, "Panama Canal Runs Smoothly One Year After Change."

277. Christopher Dickey, "Glacial Chill Settles Over Cuba's Ties with Latins," *Washington Post,* September 30, 1981.

278. *Soviet World Outlook* (August 15, 1981), p. 7.

279. "Three Points on the Map: The Socio-Political Situation and the Working People's Struggle in Panama, Malta and Malawi," *World Marxist Review* (June 1979), p. 6.

280. *La Prensa* (Panama), November 28, 1981, p. 1.

281. *La Nacion* (San Jose), May 9, 1981.

282. *La Nacion* (San Jose), May 13, 1981.

283. *Excelsior* (Mexico City), April 10, 1980.

284. FBIS, Latin America, October 30, 1981, p. S-1.

285. Ibid.

286. "Reportage on Soviet Trade Delegation Visit," FBIS, Latin America, May 21, 1981, p. B-1.

287. *New York Times,* July 12, 1981, p. 4E.

288. U.S. Arms Control and Disarmament Agency, *World Military Expenditures and Arms Transfers,* 1968–1977 (Washington, D.C.: Government Printing Office, 1979), p. 158; FBIS, Latin America, October 4, 1981, p. J–1.

289. For a more extensive discussion of these proposals see Robert S. Leiken, "Eastern Winds in Latin America," pp. 107–111, and "Reconstructing Central American Policy," *Washington Quarterly* (Winter 1982), pp. 57–60.

About the Author

Robert S. Leiken is director of the Soviet-Latin American project and a fellow in Latin American Studies at the Center for Strategic and International Studies, Georgetown University. A graduate of Harvard University, he was a Harvard Traveling Fellow at Oxford University. He has taught at Harvard and MIT and has been professor of economic history at Centro de Investigacion y Docencia Economica (C.I.D.E.) in Mexico City and of the Graduate Economics Program at the National Agricultural University at Chapingo, Mexico. He has published a widely-discussed article in *Foreign Policy* (Spring 1981) on Soviet-Latin American relations and is currently writing a book on the subject. His most recent article, "Reconstructing Central American Policy," appears in the Winter 1982 edition of *The Washington Quarterly*. Mr Leiken is also a regular contributor to *The New Republic*.

The
Washington
Papers

8 times a year, **The Washington Papers** provide policymakers with the latest and best information on the issues of the day. The advisory board of the Center for Strategic and International Studies identifies issues that underlie important forthcoming policy decisions—issues insufficiently explored—and engages leading authorities to develop analytic statements of the latest and best information.

If your library serves a public that needs the most up-to-date information on today's foreign policy issues, your library needs **The Washington Papers.** They provide you with a vital link in the formation of policy: a technical briefing on the situations that require discussion and decision at the highest government levels.

In 1982 the following papers will be published:

Saudi Arabian Modernization—J.A. Shaw and D.E. Long
"the best and most concise" *Robert G. Neumann,* former ambassador to Saudi Arabia

Soviet Energy and Western Europe—Angela Stent
"of interest to everyone interested in energy policy"
Robert B. Stobaugh, Harvard Business School

Management or Mishap: Presidential Control of Foreign Policy—Robert Hunter

The Iran-Iraq War—Stephen Grumman

Soviet Policy and Latin America—Robert Leiken

The Future of Conflict—William Taylor

Place subscription orders here!

Please enter my subscription to **The Washington Papers:**
- ☐ $35.00/year individual   ☐ $45.00/year institutional

Outside the U.S. My subscription should be sent via:
- ☐ surface mail ($7.00)   ☐ airmail ($25.00)

Name_____

Institution_____

Address_____

City_____ State_____ Zip_____

Mail to: **The Washington Papers,** Box 465, Hanover, PA 17331

- -

Order books and single issues here!

Please send me the following issues of **The Washington Papers** and/or
Praeger books:

ISBN	**Title/Author**	**Price**
_____	_____	_____
_____	_____	_____
_____	_____	_____

Invoices will include shipping, handling, and sales tax. Orders over $75.00
must be accompanied by prepayment including 5% shipping charge, 75¢
handling charge and applicable sales tax. All prices subject to change without
notice.

Name_____

Institution_____

Address_____

City_____ State_____ Zip_____

Mail to: Praeger Publishers, Box WP, 521 Fifth Avenue, New York, NY 10175